FAMILY-FRIENDLY
Knits

FAMILY-FRIENDLY
Knits

seasonal knitted garments and
accessories for children and adults

COURTNEY SPAINHOWER

INTERWEAVE.
interweave.com

CONTENTS

♡ introduction

When I first conceived this book, I had clear inspiration from my time living in Oregon, specifically my morning routine of carefully treading down to the stream to gather water to boil and washing up as best I could in the biting cold. Our days were spent collecting wild blackberries, sewing, and reading into the night by flashlight. As the sun slid down the back side of the mountain, the air became wet and stung our faces with the slow, cold fog that crept in at dusk. Each day we wore boots and long johns, and our natural curls were left to grow long and untamed. I had with me only one sweater through that time, a pale blue, gray, and white Lopi cardigan with pewter buttons that my mother gave me as a long-distance embrace and as a reminder of her own youth spent in the mountains.

My life has veered far from high altitudes and the days of such quiet living. Now, a moment of quiet between career and family is rare, and I often forget how to summon the memory of the young woman I was. I have wondered what my life would look like if I could fold it like a piece of paper, joining then and now, collapsing my quiet, nostalgic youth onto my bustling adult life with my charming husband and spirited children; that is the place where this collection was born.

Each piece carries either a slice of life then, a dollop of life now, or a sweet marriage of the two. The following pages are packed with a diverse selection of knits for men, women, and children with comfort and wearability at the forefront of their design. I've designed these pieces to be enticing to knit and functional for daily life.

The scope of skill level and techniques will engage beginning and experienced knitters alike, each pattern featuring easy-to-memorize stitches, logical construction, and little or no finishing. If you find yourself confronted with something completely unknown to you, I encourage you to dive in. All the information you need to complete these projects is tucked within these pages.

I've done some very careful planning for men and children here because they are both famously difficult to knit for, squawking at the first sign of itchy wool, constricting necklines or sleeves, and overworked stitching. Because color is extremely personal, I stress using hues and tones that kids will love to show off and that men will feel comfortable in. The women's pieces are more daring, peppered with rich colors and textures with construction and style reigning.

Knitting is a test of endurance, and for those with less experience, larger pieces should be worked up to; however, I stress to new knitters the importance of pushing themselves and attempting a pattern that speaks to them even if they aren't confident in their skill. As a knitting instructor, I am always pleased to see the spark behind knitters' eyes when they realize how capable they truly are.

THE
PROJECTS

SUMMER LACE *pullover* ⌘

I count down the days until summer. Few things bring me more joy than sitting in the sun watching my girls pluck weeds from the garden and squeal at the sight of a slug. Many knitters put away their needles for the season, but I'm no seasonal knitter. This pullover features plant fiber paired with simple lace and is perfect for hot summer days. The piece is worked from the top down, seamlessly, with saddle shoulders, and incorporates short-rows to create gently sloping arcs.

finished size

BUST CIRCUMFERENCE: About 33½ (35¾, 37½, 38½, 41, 44¼)" (85 [90.5, 95, 98, 104, 112.5] cm).

Pullover shown measures 35¾" (90.5 cm).

yarn

DK (#3 Light).

SHOWN HERE: Classic Elite Firefly (75% viscose, 25% linen; 155 yd [142 m]/3/4 oz [50 g]): #7706 linum (A), 2 (2, 2, 3, 3, 3) skeins; #7750 leopard's bane (B), 4 (5, 5, 5, 6, 6) skeins.

needles

Size U.S. 5 (3.75 mm): 16" (40 cm) and 32" (80 cm) circular (cir) and set of 4 or 5 double-pointed (dpn).

Adjust needle size if necessary to obtain the correct gauge.

notions

Markers (m); stitch holders or waste yarn; tapestry needle.

gauge

23 sts and 30 rnds = 4" (10 cm) in stockinette stitch, worked in rnds.

21 sts and 32 rows = 4" (10 cm) in Little Diamond Lace chart, worked in rows.

24 sts and 37 rows = 4" (10 cm) in garter stitch, worked in rows.

notes

✻ For this pullover, stitches are cast on at the neckline, then the left saddle tab is worked, stitches are picked up along the back side of the left tab, the back neckline stitches are knit, then the right saddle tab is worked. Stitches are picked up along the front side of the right tab, the front neckline stitches are knit, then stitches are picked up along the front side of the left tab. The front of the pullover is worked to the underarm then held while the back is worked. The front and back pieces are joined and worked in the round, and finished simply in 2×2 rib. Pleats are worked at the underarms when working the armbands.

✻ Schematic shows the bust measurements while blocking. The pleats worked while knitting the armbands (shown on page 17) decrease stitches, which results in the finished bust circumference given under Finished Size.

stitch guide

Sskpo

Ssk, then place the st back on the left needle, lift the second st on the left needle over the ssk loop, then return the ssk loop to the right needle.

1×1 Rib *(multiple of 2 sts)*

RND 1: *K1, p1 rep from *.

Rep Rnd 1 for patt.

2×2 Rib *(multiple of 4 sts)*

RND 1: *K2, p2; rep from *.

Rep Rnd 1 for patt.

LITTLE DIAMOND LACE CHART

		O	⅄	O			O	/	7
	O	/		\	O		O	/	5
\	O				O	⅄	O		3
	\	O		O	/		\	O	1

☐ knit on RS; purl on WS

O yo

/ k2tog

\ ssk

⅄ sskpo (see Stitch Guide)

☐ pattern repeat

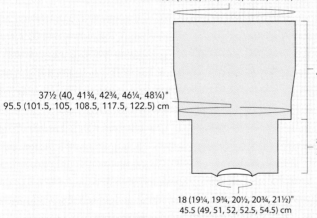

41 (43½, 45¼, 46¼, 49¾, 51¾)"
104 (110.5, 115, 117.5, 126.5, 131.5) cm

16 (16, 16½, 17, 17, 17½)"
40.5 (40.5, 42, 43, 43, 44.5) cm

37½ (40, 41¾, 42¾, 46¼, 48¼)"
95.5 (101.5, 105, 108.5, 117.5, 122.5) cm

8½ (8¾, 9, 10¼, 10¼, 10½)"
21.5 (22, 23, 26, 26, 26.5) cm

18 (19¼, 19¾, 20½, 20¾, 21½)"
45.5 (49, 51, 52, 52.5, 54.5) cm

Front: 14½ (15½, 16¾, 16¾, 16¾, 18)"
37 (39.5, 42.5, 42.5, 42.5, 45.5) cm

Back: 14½ (14½, 14½, 15½, 15½, 16¾)"
37 (37, 37, 39.5, 39.5, 42.5) cm

NECKBAND

Using color A and shorter cir needle, CO 104 (110, 114, 118, 120, 124). Place marker (pm) for beg of rnd and join for working in the rnd, being careful not to twist sts.

Work in 1x1 rib until piece meas 1" (2.5 cm) from CO edge.

SADDLE TABS

Left Tab

NEXT RND: K12, turn.

Work in garter st (knit all sts, every row) over these 12 sts only for 36 (36, 36, 38, 38, 42) rows, ending after a RS row.

Place these 12 saddle tab sts onto st holder or waste yarn.

Right Tab

With RS facing, rotate work 90° clockwise, pick up and knit 18 (18, 18, 19, 19, 21) sts (one in each "valley" between garter bumps) along the saddle tab, k39 (40, 41, 43, 44, 46) back sts, k12, turn.

Work in garter st over the last 12 sts only for 36 (36, 36, 38, 38, 42) rows, ending after a RS row.

Place the 12 saddle tab sts onto st holder or waste yarn.

With RS facing, rotate work 90° clockwise, pick up and knit 18 (18, 18, 19, 19, 21) sts (one in each "valley" between garter bumps) along the saddle tab, k41 (46, 49, 51, 52, 54) across front, pick up and knit 18 (18, 18, 19, 19, 21) sts (one in each "valley" between garter bumps) along the left saddle tab—81 (82, 85, 89, 90, 96) sts for front; 57 (58, 59, 62, 63, 67) sts for back.

Place back sts onto st holder or waste yarn and cont working back and forth in rows on front sts only.

FRONT

Sizes 33½ (38½)" only

DEC ROW: (WS) P2tog, purl to end—76 (88) sts.

Sizes 41 (44¼)" only

DEC ROW: (WS) P2tog, purl to last 2 sts, p2tog—88 (94) sts.

Size 35¾" only

Purl 1 WS row.

Size 37½" only

INC ROW: (WS) P1, M1P (see Glossary), p41, M1P, purl to last st, M1P, p1—88 sts.

All Sizes

Work Rows 1–8 of Little Diamond Lace chart 4 (4, 4, 5, 5, 5) times.

Right Bust Shaping

Shape bust darts with no-wrap short-rows (see Glossary) as foll:

SHORT-ROW 1: (RS) K24 (26, 28, 30, 30, 32), turn so WS is facing; (WS) sl 1 st purlwise with yarn in front (pwise wyf), purl to end.

SHORT-ROW 2: K22 (24, 26, 28, 28, 30), turn so WS is facing; (WS) sl 1 st pwise wyf, purl to end.

SHORT-ROW 3: Knit to 2 sts before gap, turn so WS is facing; (WS) sl 1 st pwise wyf, purl to end.

Rep the last short-row 9 (10, 11, 12, 12, 13) more times—2 sts rem unwrapped at armhole edge.

NEXT ROW: (RS) Knit to end, closing gaps as you come to them.

Left Bust Shaping

Shape bust darts with no-turn short-rows as foll:

SHORT-ROW 1: (WS) P24 (26, 28, 30, 30, 32), turn so RS is facing; (RS) sl 1 st pwise with yarn in back (wyb), knit to end.

SHORT-ROW 2: P22 (24, 26, 28, 28, 30), turn so RS is facing; (RS) sl 1 st pwise wyb, knit to end.

SHORT-ROW 3: Purl to 2 sts before gap, turn so RS is facing; (RS) sl 1 st pwise wyb, knit to end.

Rep the last short-row 9 (10, 11, 12, 12, 13) more times—2 sts rem unwrapped at armhole edge.

NEXT ROW: (WS) Purl to end, closing gaps as you come to them. Break color A.

Change to color B.

Knit 2 rows, ending after a WS row.

Place sts onto st holder or waste yarn and set aside. Break yarn.

BACK

Return 57 (58, 59, 62, 63, 67) held back sts to longer cir needle and join color A preparing to work a RS row. Knit to end, then pick up and knit 18 (18, 18, 19, 19, 21) sts in each "valley" between garter bumps along right saddle tab—75 (76, 77, 81, 82, 88) sts.

Sizes 33½ (38½)" only

INC ROW: (WS) P1, M1P, purl to end—76 (82) sts.

Sizes 35¾ (41, 44¼)" only

Purl 1 WS row.

Size 37½" only

DEC ROW: (WS) P2tog, purl to end—76 sts.

All Sizes

Work Rows 1–8 of Little Diamond Lace chart 7 (7, 7, 8, 8, 9) times.

Work even in St st (knit on RS, purl on WS) for ¼ (½, ¾, 1, 1, 1¼)" (0.6 [1.3, 2, 2.5, 2.5, 0.6] cm), ending after a WS row. Break color A.

Change to color B.

Knit 2 rows, ending after a WS row.

BODY

JOINING RND: (RS) K76 (76, 76, 82, 82, 88) back sts, turn so WS is facing, then use the cable method (see Glossary) to CO 16 (18, 19, 19, 24, 24), pm for side, then CO another 16 (18, 19, 19, 24, 24) sts, turn so RS is facing, return 76 (82, 88, 88, 88, 94) held front sts to empty end of needle and knit across, turn so WS is facing, then use the cable method to CO 16 (18, 19, 19, 24, 24), pm for beg of rnd, then CO another 16 (18, 19, 19, 24, 24) sts—216 (230, 240, 246, 266, 278) sts.

Turn so RS is facing and join to work in the rnd.

Work even in St st (knit all sts, every rnd) until piece meas 3" (7.5 cm) from joining rnd.

Shape Sides

INC RND: K1, *M1R (see Glossary), knit to 1 st before m, M1L (see Glossary), k1, sl m; rep from * once more—4 sts inc'd.

Knit 7 rnds even.

Rep the last 8 rnds 4 more times—236 (250, 260, 266, 286, 298) sts.

Work even in St st until piece meas 14 (14, 14½, 15, 15, 15½)" (35.5 [35.5, 37, 38, 38, 39.5] cm) from joining rnd.

Sizes 35¾ (38½, 41, 44¼)" only

DEC RND: K1, k2tog, knit to m, slm, k2tog, knit to end—234 (248, 260, 284) sts.

Sizes 33½ (37½)" only

Knit 1 rnd.

All Sizes

Work in 2x2 rib for 2" (5 cm).

BO all sts in patt.

FINISHING

Block piece to measurements.

Armbands

With RS facing, using color A and dpn, beg at center of underarm CO sts, pick up and knit 16 (18, 19, 19, 24, 24) sts along CO sts, 20 (20, 24, 28, 28, 30) sts evenly along selvedge edge to held saddle tab sts, return 12 saddle tab sts to empty end of needle and knit across, pick up and knit 20 (20, 24, 28, 28, 30) sts evenly along selvedge edge to CO sts, then pick up and knit 16 (18, 19, 19, 24, 24) sts in rem CO sts—84 (88, 98, 106, 116, 120) sts. Pm for beg of rnd and join to work in the rnd.

Purl 1 rnd.

Shape Pleats

PLEAT RND: Place 6 sts onto a dpn and hold to the back, place next 6 sts onto a second dpn and hold to the back. Hold the 2 dpn in the back of the work so the first dpn is in the back, the second dpn is in the center, and the working needle is in the front (like a Z). [Knit through first st on each needle, knitting them together] 6 times, knit to last 18 sts, place next 6 sts onto a dpn and hold to the front, place next 6 sts onto a second dpn and hold to the front. Hold the 2 dpn in the front of the work so the first dpn is in the front, the second dpn is in the center, and the working needle is in the back (like a Z). [Knit through first st on each needle, knitting them together] 6 times—60 (64, 74, 82, 92, 96) sts rem.

[Purl 1 rnd, knit 1 rnd] 3 times.

BO all sts loosely.

Work second armband the same as the first.

Using tapestry needle, weave in all ends neatly. Block again if desired.

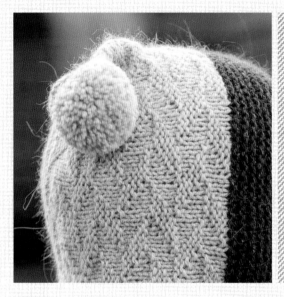

GRAIN *hood* ♡

A simple hood is one of my family's cool-weather must-haves. My girls have always loved these whimsical toppers that cover their ears and tie securely. In fact, my youngest has never wanted to part with a single one I've knit over the years. She passed the smaller ones down to her baby dolls. Seaming becomes tedious after a while, so the hood is cast on at the center back using the two-needle cast-on method and is worked flat in one piece from back to front.

finished size

About 9½ (11½, 13½, 16¾)" (24 [29, 34.5, 42.5] cm) bottom edge width.

TO FIT: 3–5y (6–8y, Adult S, Adult L).

Hat shown measures 11½" (29 cm).

yarn

Worsted (#4 Medium).

SHOWN HERE: Hikoo Kenzie (50% New Zealand merino wool, 25% nylon, 10% angora, 10% alpaca, 5% silk noils; 160 yd [146 m]/3/4 oz [50 g]): #1000 pavlova (A), 1 (1, 1, 2) skeins; #1004 beetroot (B), 1 skein.

needles

Size U.S. 7 (4.5 mm): 32" (80 cm) circular (cir) and set of 2 double-pointed (dpn).

Adjust needle size if necessary to obtain the correct gauge.

notions

Marker (m); stitch holder or waste yarn; tapestry needle.

gauge

20 sts and 34 rows = 4" (10 cm) in Double Parallelogram chart.

notes

✳ Circular needle is used to accommodate large number of sts. Do not join; work back and forth in rows.

✳ This hat is cast on at the center back using a two-needle cast-on (see Glossary) that may take a couple of attempts before you feel comfortable working. I suggest casting on a swatch size to get into the rhythm of this unique method.

DOUBLE PARALLELOGRAM
CHART A

DOUBLE PARALLELOGRAM
CHART B

9
7
5
3
1

9
7
5
3
1

☐ knit on RS; purl on WS

• ⃞ purl on RS; knit on WS

☐ pattern repeat

BODY

Using color A and two-needle cast-on (see Glossary), CO 40 (48, 56, 64) sts to each end of cir needle, placing a marker between them.

EST PATT: Work Row 1 of Double Parallelogram chart A to m, sl m, then work Row 1 of Double Parallelogram chart B to end.

Cont working in patt as est until Rows 1–10 of charts are completed 3 (3, 3, 4) times, then rep Rows 1–4 0 (1, 1, 1) more time(s).

Remove m and break yarn.

TRIM

Change to color B.

Work in garter st (knit all sts, every row) for 1¼ (1¾, 2¾, 3¼)" (3.2 [4.5, 7, 8.5] cm), ending after a WS row.

NEXT ROW: (RS) K3 and place these sts onto st holder or waste yarn, BO 34 (42, 50, 58) sts, knit to end—3 sts rem.

TIES

Transfer 3 sts to dpn and work in I-cord (see Glossary) for 10 (10, 12, 12)" (25.5 [25.5, 30.5, 30.5] cm). Break yarn.

Work second tie the same as the first using 3 held sts.

FINISHING

If desired, make a pom-pom (see Glossary) with color A and secure it to the point.

Using tapestry needle, weave in all ends neatly.

Block to measurements.

LIND**Y** *yoke pullover*

Winter weather makes me think of cables and wool—a classic pairing to cozy up in during the long, cold nights of the season. This simple yoke sweater knits up simply and quickly with subtle cable details in the front and on the shoulders, making it as comfortable as, but a little nicer looking, than a sweatshirt-style sweater. It will surely become a cold-weather staple.

finished size

CHEST CIRCUMFERENCE: About 35½ (39, 42¾, 46¼)" (90 [99, 108.5, 117.5] cm).

Pullover shown measures 39" (99 cm).

yarn

Worsted (#4 Medium).

SHOWN HERE: Tahki Yarns Tara Tweed (80% wool, 20% nylon; 122 yd [113 m]/1 ¾ oz [50 g]): #022 smoke tweed (A), 8 (9, 10, 11) balls.

Lace (#1 Super Fine).

SHOWN HERE: Madelinetosh Lace (100% superwash merino wool; 950 yd [868 m]/4 oz [120 g]): ink (B), 1 (1, 2, 2) hanks.

needles

Size U.S. 7 (4.5 mm): 16" (40 cm) and 32" (80 cm) circular (cir) and set of 4 or 5 double-pointed (dpn).

Adjust needle size if necessary to obtain the correct gauge.

notions

Markers (m); cable needle (cn); stitch holders or waste yarn; tapestry needle.

gauge

18 sts and 27 rnds = 4" (10 cm) in St st, worked in rnds with 1 strand of each color A and color B held together.

19 sts and 28 rnds = 4" (10 cm) in St st, worked in rnds with 1 strand of color A only.

12 sts = 1½" (3.8 cm) in Cable Panel chart.

note

❋ This pullover is worked from the bottom up holding two strands together to create marled fabric on the body and sleeves. Once joined for the yoke, continue with one strand of color A only and work cables and decreases as outlined.

stitch guide

4/4LC

Sl 4 sts to cn and hold in front, k4, k4 from cn.

4/4RC

Sl 4 sts to cn and hold in back, k4, k4 from cn.

1×1 Rib *(multiple of 2 sts)*

RND 1: *K1, p1 rep from * to end.

Rep Rnd 1 for patt.

CABLE PANEL CHART

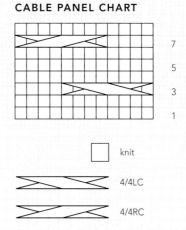

7
5
3
1

□ knit

4/4LC

4/4RC

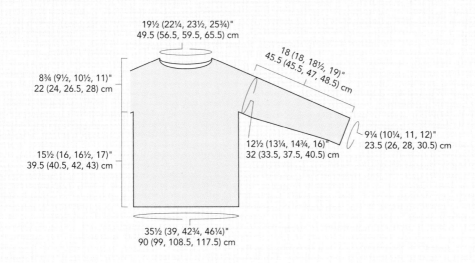

19½ (22¼, 23½, 25¾)"
49.5 (56.5, 59.5, 65.5) cm

18 (18, 18½, 19)"
45.5 (45.5, 47, 48.5) cm

8¾ (9½, 10½, 11)"
22 (24, 26.5, 28) cm

12½ (13¼, 14¾, 16)"
32 (33.5, 37.5, 40.5) cm

9¼ (10¼, 11, 12)"
23.5 (26, 28, 30.5) cm

15½ (16, 16½, 17)"
39.5 (40.5, 42, 43) cm

35½ (39, 42¾, 46¼)"
90 (99, 108.5, 117.5) cm

lindy yoke pullover

BODY

Holding 1 strand of each color A and color B together and using longer cir needle, CO 160 (176, 192, 208) sts. Place marker (pm) for beg of rnd and join to work in the rnd, being careful not to twist sts.

Work in 2x2 rib until piece meas 1¾" (4.5 cm) from CO edge.

Work even in St st (knit all sts, every rnd) until piece meas 15½ (16, 16½, 17)" (39.5 [40.5, 42, 43] cm) from CO edge, knitting to last 4 (5, 5, 6) sts on last rnd. Place rem 4 (5, 5, 6) sts and the first 4 (5, 5, 6) sts of next rnd onto st holder or waste yarn for underarm—152 (166, 182, 196) sts rem.

Break strand of color B, but keep color A attached and set aside, keeping sts on cir needle.

SLEEVES

Holding 1 strand of each color A and color B together, and using dpn, CO 42 (46, 50, 54) sts. Divide sts evenly over 3 or 4 needles. Pm for beg of rnd and join to work in the rnd, being careful not to twist sts.

Work in 1x1 rib until piece meas 2" (5 cm) from CO edge.

Shape Sleeve

Knit 12 (11, 11, 11) rnds.

INC RND: K1, M1L (see Glossary), knit to last st, M1R (see Glossary), k1—2 sts inc'd.

Rep the last 13 (12, 12, 12) rnds 6 (6, 7, 8) more times—56 (60, 66, 72) sts.

Work even in St st until piece meas 18 (18, 18½, 19)" (45.5 [45.5, 47, 48.5] cm) from CO edge, knitting to last 4 (5, 5, 6) sts on last rnd. Place these sts and the first 4 (5, 5, 6) sts of next rnd onto waste yarn—48 (50, 56, 60) sts rem.

Place rem sts onto separate st holder or waste yarn. Break yarn and set aside.

Make second sleeve the same as the first, keeping 48 (50, 56, 60) sts on dpn. Break yarn.

Yoke

JOINING RND: Cont with longer cir needle and single strand of color A attached to body, k48 (50, 56, 60) sleeve sts, k72 (78, 86, 92) body sts for front, place next 8 (10, 10, 12) body sts onto st holder or waste yarn for underarm, return 48 (50, 56, 60) held sts from the other sleeve to empty needle, then knit across, knit rem 72 (78, 86, 92) body sts for back—240 (256, 284, 304) sts.

Place markers for cable panels as foll:

NEXT RND: K18 (19, 22, 24), *pm, k12, pm, k48 (52, 59, 64); rep from * once more, pm, k12, pm, k90 (97, 108, 116) to end.

EST PATT: *Knit to m, sl m, work Cable Panel chart to next m, sl m; rep from * 2 more times, knit to end.

Cont working even as est for 15 (16, 18, 19) more rnds.

Shape Yoke

note: Change to shorter cir needle when sts no longer fit comfortably on longer cir needle.

DEC RND 1: K0 (1, 4, 0), [k4, k2tog] 3 (3, 3, 4) times to m, sl m, work Cable Panel chart to m, sl m, *k0 (4, 5, 4), [k4, k2tog] 8 (8, 9, 10) times to m, sl m, work Cable Panel chart to m, sl m; rep from * once more, k0 (1, 0, 2), [k4, k2tog] 15 (16, 18, 19) times to end—206 (221, 245, 261) sts rem.

Work 14 (15, 16, 17) rnds even in patt as est.

DEC RND 2: K0 (1, 4, 0), [k3, k2tog] 3 (3, 3, 4) times to m, sl m, work Cable Panel chart to m, sl m, *k0 (4, 0, 4), [k3, k2tog] 8 (8, 10, 10) times to m, sl m, work Cable Panel chart to m, sl m; rep from * once more, k0 (1, 0, 2), [k3, k2tog] 15 (16, 18, 19) times to end—172 (186, 204, 218) sts rem.

Work 6 (7, 8, 9) rnds even in patt as est.

DEC RND 3: K0 (1, 4, 0), [k2, k2tog] 3 (3, 3, 4) times to m, sl m, work Cable Panel chart to m, sl m, *k0 (4, 0, 4), [k2, k2tog] 8 (8, 10, 10) times to m, sl m, work Cable Panel chart to m, sl m; rep from * once more, k0 (1, 0, 2), [k2, k2tog] 15 (16, 18, 19) times to end—138 (151, 163, 175) sts rem.

Work 6 (7, 8, 9) rnds even in patt as est.

DEC RND 4: K0 (1, 4, 0), [k1, k2tog] 3 (3, 3, 4) times to m, sl m, work Cable Panel chart to m, sl m, *k0 (4, 0, 4), [k1, k2tog] 8 (8, 10, 10) times to m, sl m, work Cable Panel chart to m, sl m; rep from * once more, k0 (1, 0, 2), [k1, k2tog] 15 (16, 18, 19) times to end—104 (116, 122, 132) sts rem.

Knit even 1 rnd.

Work in 1x1 rib for 1" (2.5 cm).

BO all sts in patt.

FINISHING

Return 8 (10, 10, 12) held underarm sts from body and sleeve to dpn. Use tapestry needle to graft them together using Kitchener st (see Glossary). Weave in all ends neatly.

Block piece to measurements.

ELLEN *saddle gansey*

When cooler air begins its descent, I still keep my windows cracked open so that I can savor the last bits of fresh air sweeping past the sills. A hot cup of tea and cozy sweater become constant companions with the welcome chill. This gansey is constructed in one piece from the top down with saddle shoulders that merge seamlessly with the sleeve. Unlike many traditional ganseys, Ellen incorporates simple no-wrap short-rows in the sleeve cap to create a neat fit in the shoulders.

finished size

BUST CIRCUMFERENCE: About 32¾ (35, 36¾, 38½, 40¼, 42¾, 43½)" (83 [89, 93.5, 98, 102, 108.5, 110.5] cm).

Pullover shown measures 35" (89 cm).

yarn

Worsted (#4 Medium).

SHOWN HERE: Quince and Co. Owl (50% American wool, 50% alpaca; 120 yd [110 m]/50 g): #322 hemlock, 9 (10, 10, 11, 11, 12, 12) hanks.

needles

Size U.S. 7 (4.5 mm): 16" (40 cm) and 32" (80 cm) circular (cir) and set of 4 or 5 double-pointed (dpn).

Adjust needle size if necessary to obtain the correct gauge.

notions

Markers (m); stitch holders or waste yarn; tapestry needle.

gauge

19 sts and 27 rnds = 4" (10 cm) in St st, worked in rnds.

notes

* It is recommended to use a contrasting color stitch marker for the beg of rnd and saddle, to easily tell them apart from other markers used.

* This pullover is worked in one piece from the top down. Saddles are created by increasing on each side of garter shoulder panels every round—be careful to complete these increases to ensure proper shoulder shaping.

stitch guide

Broken Rib *(multiple of 2 sts + 1)*

RND 1: *K1, p1; rep from * to last st, k1.

RND 2: Knit.

Rep Rnds 1 and 2 for patt.

2×2 Rib *(multiple of 4 sts)*

RND 1: *K2, p2; rep from *.

Rep Rnd 1 for patt.

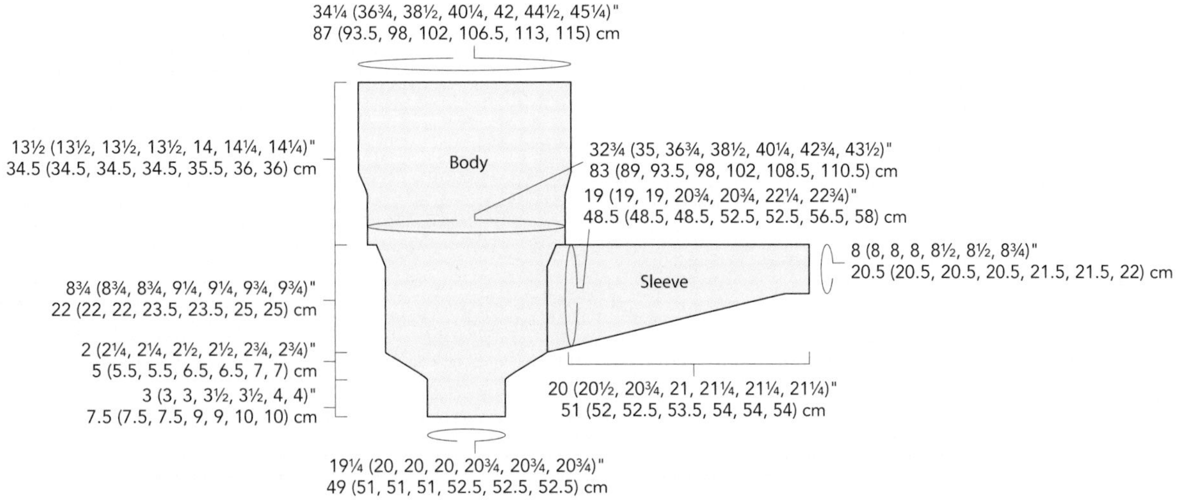

34¼ (36¾, 38½, 40¼, 42, 44½, 45¼)"
87 (93.5, 98, 102, 106.5, 113, 115) cm

13½ (13½, 13½, 13½, 14, 14¼, 14¼)"
34.5 (34.5, 34.5, 34.5, 35.5, 36, 36) cm

Body

32¾ (35, 36¾, 38½, 40¼, 42¾, 43½)"
83 (89, 93.5, 98, 102, 108.5, 110.5) cm

19 (19, 19, 20¾, 20¾, 22¼, 22¾)"
48.5 (48.5, 48.5, 52.5, 52.5, 56.5, 58) cm

8 (8, 8, 8, 8½, 8½, 8¾)"
20.5 (20.5, 20.5, 20.5, 21.5, 21.5, 22) cm

8¾ (8¾, 8¾, 9¼, 9¼, 9¾, 9¾)"
22 (22, 22, 23.5, 23.5, 25, 25) cm

Sleeve

2 (2¼, 2¼, 2½, 2½, 2¾, 2¾)"
5 (5.5, 5.5, 6.5, 6.5, 7, 7) cm

3 (3, 3, 3½, 3½, 4, 4)"
7.5 (7.5, 7.5, 9, 9, 10, 10) cm

20 (20½, 20¾, 21, 21¼, 21¼, 21¼)"
51 (52, 52.5, 53.5, 54, 54, 54) cm

19¼ (20, 20, 20, 20¾, 20¾, 20¾)"
49 (51, 51, 51, 52.5, 52.5, 52.5) cm

ellen saddle gansey

YOKE

Collar

With shorter cir needle, CO 91 (95, 95, 95, 99, 99, 99). Place marker (pm) for beg of rnd and join to work in the rnd, being careful not to twist sts.

SET-UP RND: P10 for first saddle tab, pm, k9, pm, p20 (22, 22, 22, 24, 24, 24), pm, k9 for front, pm, p10 for second saddle tab, k33 (35, 35, 35, 37, 37, 37) for back.

EST BROKEN RIB: *Work in garter st (knit 1 rnd, purl 1 rnd) to m, sl m, work in broken rib to m, sl m; rep from * 2 more times.

Cont working even as est for 9 more rnds.

EST PATT: *Work in garter st to m, sl m, work in St st (knit all sts, every rnd) to m, sl m; rep from * 2 more times.

Cont working even as est until piece meas 3 (3, 3, 3½, 3½, 4, 4)" (7.5 [7.5, 7.5, 9, 9, 10, 10] cm) from CO edge, ending after a purl rnd of garter st.

Shape Shoulders

INC RND: Work in garter st to m, sl m, k1, M1L (see Glossary), knit to next m, sl m, work in garter st to next m, sl m, knit to 1 st before next m, M1R (see Glossary), k1, sl m, work in garter st to next m, sl m, k1, M1L, knit to 1 st before last m, M1R, k1—4 sts inc'd.

Rep last rnd 12 (14, 16, 16, 16, 18, 18) times—143 (155, 163, 163, 167, 175, 175) sts; 10 sts each saddle, 64 (70, 74, 74, 76, 80, 80) sts for front and 59 (65, 69, 69, 71, 75, 75) sts for back.

Place first 10 saddle tab sts onto st holder or waste yarn, place 64 (70, 74, 74, 76, 80, 80) front sts onto a separate st holder or waste yarn, place next 10 saddle tab sts onto st holder or waste yarn. Cont working back and forth on 59 (65, 69, 69, 71, 75, 75) back sts only.

BACK

Work even in St st (knit on RS, purl on WS) until piece meas 7½ (7½, 7½, 8, 8, 8½, 8½)" (19 [19, 19, 20.5, 20.5, 21.5, 21.5] cm) from shoulder, ending after a WS row.

Shape Armholes

INC ROW: (RS) K1, M1L, knit to last st, M1R, k1—2 sts inc'd.

Purl 1 WS row.

Rep the last 2 rows 3 more times—67 (73, 77, 77, 77, 83, 83) sts.

Break yarn and place back sts onto st holder or waste yarn.

FRONT

Transfer 64 (70, 74, 74, 76, 80, 80) held front sts onto longer cir needle and rejoin yarn preparing to work a WS row. Do not join; work back and forth in rows.

Work in St st and garter st as est until piece meas 7½ (7½, 7½, 8, 8, 8½, 8½)" (19 [19, 19, 20.5, 20.5, 21.5, 21.5] cm) from shoulder, ending after a WS row.

Shape Armholes

INC ROW: (RS) K1, M1L, knit m, sl m, work in garter st to next m, sl m, knit to last st, M1R, k1—2 sts inc'd.

NEXT ROW: (WS) Purl to m, sl m, knit to next m, sl m, purl to end.

Rep the last 2 rows 3 more times—72 (78, 82, 82, 84, 88, 88) sts. Do not break yarn.

BODY

JOINING RND: With RS facing, work 72 (78, 82, 82, 84, 88, 88) front sts as est, use the backward-loop method (see Glossary) to CO 4 (4, 4, 6, 7, 8, 9) sts, pm for side, CO another 4 (4, 4, 6, 7, 8, 9) sts, transfer 67 (73, 77, 77, 79, 83, 83) held back sts to empty end of needle and knit across, use the backward-loop method to CO 4 (4, 4, 6, 7, 8, 9) sts, pm for beg of rnd, then CO another 4 (4, 4, 6, 7, 8, 9) sts, join to work in the rnd—155 (167, 175, 183, 191, 203, 207) sts.

Work even in St st until piece meas 4" (10 cm) from joining rnd.

Shape Sides

INC RND 1: *K1, M1L, work as est to 1 st before next m, M1R, k1, sl m; rep from * once more—4 sts inc'd.

Knit 6 rnds even.

Rep the last 7 rnds once more—163 (175, 183, 191, 199, 211, 215) sts.

Work even in St st until piece meas 12 (12, 12, 12, 12½, 12¾, 12¾)" (30.5 [30.5, 30.5, 30.5, 31.5, 32, 32] cm) from joining rnd.

INC RND 2: K1, M1L, work to end as est—164 (176, 184, 192, 200, 212, 216) sts.

Work even 2x2 rib for 1½" (3.8 cm).

BO all sts in patt.

SLEEVES

Using shorter cir needle and with RS facing, beg at center of underarm CO sts, pick up and knit 4 (4, 4, 6, 7, 8, 9) sts from underarm, 36 (36, 36, 38, 37, 40, 40) sts along selvedge edge to saddle sts, pm, return 10 held saddle tab sts to empty end of needle, then work them in garter st as est, pick up and knit 36 (36, 36, 38, 37, 40, 40) sts along selvedge edge to underarm, then pick up and knit rem 4 (4, 4, 6, 7, 8, 9) underarm sts—90 (90, 90, 98, 98, 106, 108) sts. Pm for beg of rnd, join for working in the rnd.

Shape Cap

Shape cap with no-wrap short-rows (see Glossary) as foll:

SHORT-ROW 1: (RS) Knit to m, sl m work in garter st to next m, sl m, k10, turn so WS is facing; (WS) sl 1 st purlwise with yarn in front (wyf), purl to m, sl m, work in garter st to next m, sl m, p10, turn so RS is facing.

SHORT-ROW 2: (RS) Sl 1 st pwise with yarn in back (wyb), knit to m, sl m work in garter st to next m, sl m, knit to 2 sts before gap, turn so WS is facing; (WS) sl 1 st pwise wyf, purl to m, sl m, work in garter st to next m, sl m, purl to 2 sts before gap, turn so RS is facing.

Rep the last short-row 3 more times.

NEXT RND: (RS) Sl 1 st pwise wyb, knit to m, sl m, work in garter st to next m, sl m, knit to end of rnd closing gaps as you come to them.

Work even 1 rnd as est closing rem gaps as you come to them.

Cont working even as est until piece meas 2" (5 cm) from underarm.

Shape Sleeve

note: Change to dpn when sts no longer fit comfortably on cir needle.

Work even as est for 3 (3, 3, 2, 2, 2, 2) rnds.

DEC RND: Knit to 3 sts before m, ssk, k1, sl m, work in garter st to next m, sl m, k1, k2tog, knit to end—2 sts dec'd.

Rep the last 4 (4, 4, 3, 3, 3, 3) rnds 21 (18, 16, 5, 0, 11, 15) more times—46 (52, 56, 86, 96, 82, 76) sts rem.

[Work even as est for 4 (4, 4, 3, 3, 3, 3) rnds, then rep dec rnd] 4 (7, 9, 24, 28, 20, 17) times—38 (38, 38, 38, 40, 42, 42) sts rem.

Cont working even as est until piece meas 18 (18½, 18¾, 19, 19¼, 19¼, 19¼)" (45.5 [47, 47.5, 48.5, 49, 49, 49] cm) from underarm, ending after a knit rnd of garter st.

EST BROKEN RIB: [K1, p1] to m, sl m, purl to next m, sl m, [k1, p1] to end.

NEXT RND: Knit.

Rep the last 2 rnds for 2" (5 cm).

BO all sts loosely.

Work second sleeve the same as the first.

FINISHING

Using tapestry needle, weave in all ends neatly.

Block to measurements.

AILERON *shawl cardigan* ✤

Shawl cardigans are my most-worn pieces in the spring and fall. The gentle drape and simple construction make these sweaters perfect for light layering, and they can range from casual to elegant. The Aileron (French for "little wing") is named for the angel wing cables between the shoulder blades. This is a great introduction to shawl cardigans because it's just a rectangle with openings for the armholes; sleeves are shaped using easy no-wrap short-rows.

finished size

About 14½ (15, 15½, 16, 16½, 17, 17½)" (37 [38, 39.5, 40.5, 42, 43, 44.5] cm) across back.

To fit about 32 (34, 36, 38, 40, 42, 44)" (81.5 [86.5, 91.5, 96.5, 101.5, 106.5, 112] cm) bust circumference.

Cardigan shown measures 15" (38 cm).

yarn

Fingering (#1 Super Fine).

SHOWN HERE: Malabrigo Yarn Sock (100% superwash merino wool; 440 yd [402 m]/1½ oz [100 g]): #801 Botticelli red, 4 (4, 4, 5, 5, 5, 5) skeins.

needles

Size U.S. 5 (3.75 mm): 32" (80 cm) circular (cir) and set of 4 or 5 double-pointed (dpn).

Adjust needle size if necessary to obtain the correct gauge.

notions

Markers (m); removable marker; cable needle (cn); waste yarn; tapestry needle.

gauge

28 sts and 43 rows = 4" (10 cm) in St st.

notes

* Circular needle is used to accommodate large number of sts. Do not join; work back and forth in rows.

* It's recommended to use a contrasting color stitch marker for the Angel Wing Cable chart markers, to easily tell them apart from other markers used.

* This cardigan is cast on at the left front and worked sideways to armholes where waste yarn is knit into the fabric to be removed later. The remaining cardigan is knit even to the right front edge. Once waste yarn is removed, live stitches are transferred onto dpn and shoulder caps for sleeves are formed using no-wrap short-rows.

stitch guide

4/4LC

Sl 4 sts to cn and hold in front, k4, k4 from cn.

4/4RC

Sl 4 sts to cn and hold in back, k4, k4 from cn.

Broken Rib *(multiple of 2 sts)*

ROW 1: (WS) *K1, p1; rep from *.

ROW 2: (RS) Knit.

Rep Rows 1 and 2 for patt.

2×2 Rib *(multiple of 4 sts)*

ROW 1: *K2, p2; rep from *.

ROW 2: *P2, k2; rep from *.

Rep Rows 1 and 2 for patt.

ANGEL WING CABLE CHART

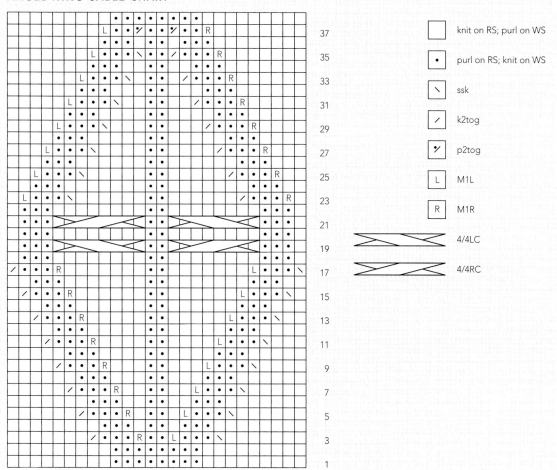

☐		knit on RS; purl on WS
•		purl on RS; knit on WS
\		ssk
/		k2tog
✔		p2tog
L		M1L
R		M1R

4/4LC

4/4RC

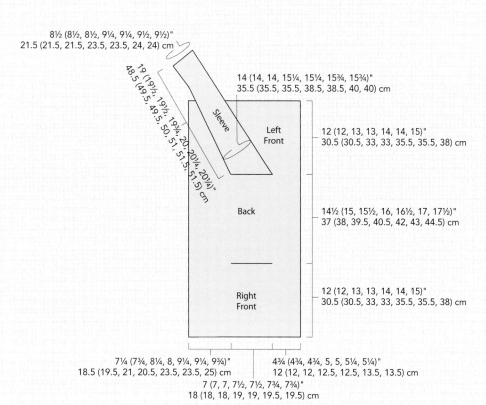

8½ (8½, 8½, 9¼, 9¼, 9½, 9½)"
21.5 (21.5, 21.5, 23.5, 23.5, 24, 24) cm

19 (19½, 19½, 19¾, 20, 20¼, 20¼)"
48.5 (49.5, 49.5, 50, 51, 51.5, 51.5) cm

Sleeve

14 (14, 14, 15¼, 15¼, 15¾, 15¾)"
35.5 (35.5, 35.5, 38.5, 38.5, 40, 40) cm

Left Front

12 (12, 13, 13, 14, 14, 15)"
30.5 (30.5, 33, 33, 35.5, 35.5, 38) cm

Back

14½ (15, 15½, 16, 16½, 17, 17½)"
37 (38, 39.5, 40.5, 42, 43, 44.5) cm

Right Front

12 (12, 13, 13, 14, 14, 15)"
30.5 (30.5, 33, 33, 35.5, 35.5, 38) cm

7¼ (7¾, 8¼, 8, 9¼, 9¼, 9¾)"
18.5 (19.5, 21, 20.5, 23.5, 23.5, 25) cm

4¾ (4¾, 4¾, 5, 5, 5¼, 5¼)"
12 (12, 12, 12.5, 12.5, 13.5, 13.5) cm

7 (7, 7, 7½, 7½, 7¾, 7¾)"
18 (18, 18, 19, 19, 19.5, 19.5) cm

LEFT FRONT

Using cir needle, CO 136 (140, 144, 148, 156, 160, 164), pm, CO 14 more sts—150 (154, 158, 162, 170, 174, 178) sts. Do not join; work back and forth in rows.

EST RIB: Work in broken rib to m, sl m, work in 2x2 rib to end.

Cont working as est until piece meas 1¾" (4.5 cm) from CO edge, ending after a RS row.

EST PATT: (WS) Work in broken rib to m, sl m, p 96 (100, 104, 108, 116, 120, 124), place marker (pm), work in 2x2 rib to end.

NEXT ROW: (RS) Work in 2x2 rib to m, sl m, work in St st (knit on RS, purl on WS) to next m, sl m, work in broken rib to end.

Cont working as est until piece meas 12 (12, 13, 13, 14, 14, 15)" (30.5 [30.5, 33, 33, 35.5, 35.5, 38] cm) from CO edge, ending after a WS row.

Shape Left Armhole

NEXT ROW: (RS) Work 2x2 rib to m, sl m, k7 (7, 7, 9, 9, 11, 11), change to waste yarn and k49 (49, 49, 53, 53, 55, 55), return the 49 (49, 49, 53, 53, 55, 55) sts worked in waste yarn to the left needle and knit them with the working yarn, knit to next m, sl m, work in broken rib to end.

Work 1 row even in patt as est.

BACK

EST PATT: (RS) Work even in 2x2 rib to m, sl m, k18 (18, 18, 22, 22, 25, 25), pm for chart, work Row 1 of Angel Wing Cable chart over next 26 sts, pm, work to end as est.

NEXT ROW: Work in broken rib to m, sl m, purl to next m, sl m, work Row 2 of Angel Wing Cable chart to next m, sl m, purl to last m, sl m, work even in 2x2 rib to end.

Rep last 2 rows (repeating Rows 1 and 2 of chart only) until piece meas 5½ (5¾, 6, 6¼, 6½, 6¾, 7)" (14 [14.5, 15, 16, 16.5, 17, 18] cm) from armhole, ending after a WS row.

Cont as est, working Rows 1–38 of Angel Wing Cable chart. Place a removable m at the end of this row to use for measuring.

Cont as est, repeating only Rows 1 and 2 of chart until piece meas 5½ (5¾, 6, 6¼, 6½, 6¾, 7)" (14 [14.5, 15, 16, 16.5, 17, 18] cm) from removable m, ending after a WS row. Remove removable m.

Shape Right Armhole

Work same as for left armhole.

RIGHT FRONT

EST PATT: (RS) Work in 2x2 rib to m, sl m, work in St st to next m, sl m, work in broken rib to end.

Cont working as est until piece meas 10¼ (10¼, 11¼, 11¼, 12¼, 12¼, 13¼)" (26 [26, 28.5, 28.5, 31, 31, 33.5] cm) from right armhole, ending after a WS row.

EST RIB: (RS) Work in 2x2 rib to m, sl m, work in broken rib to end.

Cont working as est for 1¾" (4.5 cm), ending after a WS row.

BO all sts in patt to m, remove m, BO rem sts.

SLEEVES

Carefully remove waste yarn from one armhole as foll:

Beg at the underarm transfer 49 (49, 49, 53, 53, 55, 55) sts from each side onto 2 separate dpn—98 (98, 98, 106, 106, 110, 110) sts. Pm for beg of rnd, divide sts evenly over 3 or 4 dpn and join yarn to work in the rnd.

NEXT RND: K14, pm for underarm, knit to last 14 sts, pm for underarm, k14.

Shape Cap

Shape cap with no-wrap short-rows (see Glossary) as foll:

SHORT-ROW 1: (RS) K56 (56, 56, 61, 61, 65, 65), turn so WS is facing; (WS) sl 1 st purlwise with yarn in front (pwise wyf), p13 (13, 13, 15, 15, 19, 19), turn so RS is facing.

SHORT-ROW 2: (RS) Sl 1 st pwise with yarn in back (wyb), knit to gap, k1 to close gap, k1, turn so WS is facing; (WS) sl 1 st pwise wyf, purl to gap, p1 to close gap, p1, turn so RS is facing.

Rep the last short-row 27 (27, 27, 30, 30, 30, 30) more times to underarm m. Remove underarm markers.

NEXT RND: (RS) Sl 1 st pwise wyb, knit to end of rnd closing rem gap as you come to it.

Knit 1 rnd closing rem gap in rnd.

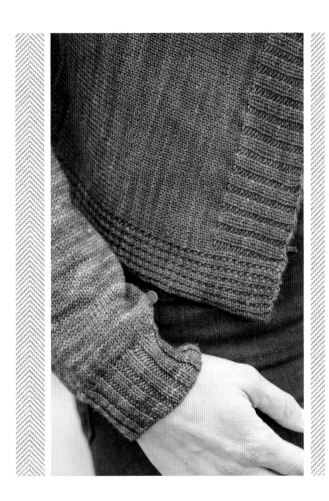

Shape Sleeve

Knit 6 (6, 6, 5, 5, 5, 5) rnds.

DEC RND: K1, k2tog, knit to last 3 sts, ssk, k1—2 sts dec'd.

Rep the last 7 (7, 7, 6, 6, 6, 6) rnds 16 (12, 12, 5, 2, 7, 7) more times—64 (72, 72, 94, 100, 94, 94) sts rem.

[Knit 7 (7, 7, 6, 6, 6, 6) rnds, then rep dec rnd] 2 (6, 6, 15, 18, 14, 14) times—60 (60, 60, 64, 64, 66, 66) sts rem.

Work even in St st (knit all sts, every rnd) until piece meas 17 (17½, 17½, 17¾, 18, 18¼, 18¼)" (43 [44.5, 44.5, 45, 45.5, 46.5, 46.5] cm) from underarm.

Work even 2x2 rib for 2" (5 cm).

BO all sts loosely.

Work second sleeve the same as the first.

FINISHING

Using tapestry needle, weave in all ends neatly.

Block to measurements.

MUST-HAVE *mitts*

Fingerless gloves are my go-to transitional accessories. My youngest has an extensive collection in a range of colors so she can grab the pair that best suits her mood. My own vanish each spring with the melting snow, so I am usually back to the needles, making a new pair each year. Though worked in fine yarn and incorporate cabling, these mitts knit up surprisingly fast for gifts. They're perfect for men, women, and children alike, and instructions are included for all.

finished size

About 4¾ (5¼, 6, 6½)" (12 [13.5, 15, 16.5] cm) hand circumference and 4¼ (5, 6, 6½" (11 [12.5, 15, 16.5] cm) length.

TO FIT: Child S (Child L, Adult S, Adult L).

Samples shown measure 4¾", 6", and 6½" (12, 15, and 16.5 cm).

yarn

Super Fine (#2 Light).

SHOWN HERE: Madelinetosh Tosh Merino Light (100% superwash merino wool; 420 yd [384 m]/1½ oz [100 g]): Adult L sample: charcoal, 1 skein; Adult S sample: Isadora, 1 skein; Child S sample: candlewick, 1 skein.

needles

Size U.S. 2 (3 mm): set of 3 or 4 double-pointed (dpn).

Adjust needle size if necessary to obtain the correct gauge.

notions

Markers (m); cable needle (cn); stitch holders or waste yarn; tapestry needle.

gauge

33 sts and 46 rnds = 4" (10 cm) in St st, worked in rnds.

18 sts = 1½" (3.8 cm) in Cable Rib chart.

note

* These mitts are worked seamlessly from the bottom up incorporating palm gusset shaping for the thumb and a cabled rib along the side.

* It is recommended to use a contrasting color stitch marker for the beg of rnd marker, to easily tell it apart from other markers used.

stitch guide

1/1RC

Sl 1 st to cn and hold in back, k1, k1 from cn.

2/1LC

Sl 2 sts to cn and hold in front, k1, k2 from cn.

2/1RC

Sl 1 st to cn and hold in back, k2, k1 from cn.

2/2LC

Sl 2 sts to cn and hold in front, k2, k2 from cn.

2/2RC

Sl 2 sts to cn and hold in back, k2, k2 from cn.

1×1 Rib *(multiple of 2 sts)*

RND 1: *K1, p1 rep from *.

Rep Rnd 1 for patt.

CABLE RIB CHART

3,4,5

□	knit
⊡	purl
⧓	2/2RC
⧓	2/2LC
⧓	2/1RC
⧓	2/1LC
⧓	1/1RC

increase on odd

M1L - M1R at end of round

MITT

Cuff

CO 40 (46, 52, 56) sts. Divide sts evenly over 3 or 4 dpn. Place marker (pm) for beg of rnd and join to work in the rnd, being careful not to twist sts.

Work in 1x1 rib until piece meas 1¼ (1½, 1¾, 1¾)" (3.2 [3.8, 4.5, 4.5] cm) from CO edge.

Gusset

SET-UP RND: K16 (20, 22, 26), pm for gusset, k3 (4, 6, 6), pm for chart, k18, pm for chart, k3 (4, 6, 6) to end.

INC RND: Knit to gusset m, sl m, M1L (see Glossary), knit to chart m, sl m, work Cable Rib chart to next chart m, sl m, knit to end, M1R (see Glossary)—2 sts inc'd.

NEXT RND: Knit to first chart m, sl m, work Cabled Rib chart to next chart m, sl m, knit to end.

Rep the last 2 rnds 7 (9, 10, 12) more times—56 (66, 74, 82) sts.

Cont working even as est for 3 (4, 4, 3) more rnds.

Hand

Remove beg of rnd m, place next 16 (20, 22, 26) sts onto st holder or waste yarn, use the backward-loop method (see Glossary) to CO 2, pm for beg of rnd, CO 2 more sts, remove m on left needle, and join to work in the rnd—44 (52, 56, 60) sts.

Cont working even as est for 7 (9, 14, 18) rnds, ending after Rnd 4 (11, 7, 3) of Cable Rib chart.

Knit 1 rnd.

Work in 1x1 rib for ½" (2 cm).

BO all sts in patt.

Work second mitt the same as the first.

THUMB

Return 16 (20, 22, 26) held sts from 1 mitt evenly onto 2 dpn. With RS facing and using a third dpn, pick up and knit 2 sts from CO sts, pm for beg of rnd, pick up and knit 2 more sts from CO sts and join to work in the rnd—20 (24, 26, 30) sts.

Knit 1 rnd.

DEC RND: *K2tog, k6 (8, 9, 11), ssk; rep from * once more—16 (20, 22, 26) sts rem.

Redistribute sts evenly over 3 dpn.

Knit 0 (2, 4, 6) rnds.

Work in 1x1 rib for ½" (2 cm).

BO all sts in patt.

Work thumb on second mitt the same as the first.

FINISHING

Using tapestry needle, weave in all ends neatly.

Block to measurements.

HALLE *yoke cardigan*

I love a heavy cardigan with ample ease for layering, and this particular piece is inspired by the heavy wool yoke cardigan my mother handed down to me to warm my bones in the Pacific Northwest. The yarn I've selected works up quickly and will keep you insulated even in wet climates. This cardigan is worked in the round from the bottom up with steeks; the sleeves are knit separately and joined to the body to complete the yoke.

finished size

About 37 (40¾, 44½, 47¼)" (94 [103.5, 113, 120] cm) bust circumference, buttoned with 1¼" (3.2 cm) overlapping buttonband.

Cardigan shown measures 37" (94 cm).

yarn

Aran (#4 Medium).

SHOWN HERE: Briggs and Little Heritage (100% pure wool; 215 yd [196 m]/113 g): #22 brown heather (A), 5 (6, 7, 7) skeins; #14 sheeps grey (B) and #36 gold (C), 1 skein each.

needles

BODY AND SLEEVES: Size U.S. 8 (5 mm): 32" (80 cm) circular (cir) and set of 4 or 5 double-pointed (dpn).

BUTTONBANDS: Size U.S. 7 (4.5 mm): 32" (80 cm) cir.

Adjust needle size if necessary to obtain the correct gauge.

notions

Markers (m); stitch holders or waste yarn; tapestry needle; eight 1" (2.5 cm) buttons; sharp scissors; needle and button thread for sewing on buttons.

BUTTONS SHOWN HERE: JHB Buttons, Coconut (1" [2.5 cm]).

gauge

17 sts and 25 rnds = 4" (10 cm) in St st with larger needle, worked in rnds.

note

✴ It is recommended to use a contrasting color stitch marker for the steek markers, to easily tell them apart from other markers used.

✴ Some of the stitches charted are to be purled rather than knit. This adds texture and visual interest to the color section.

✴ When working the color chart, work to steek sts, taking note of which st of the chart was worked last, work steek sts by alternating the colors, then cont working the color chart beg with the following st.

stitch guide

1×1 Rib *(multiple of 2 sts)*

RND 1: *K1, p1; rep from *.

Rep Rnd 1 for patt.

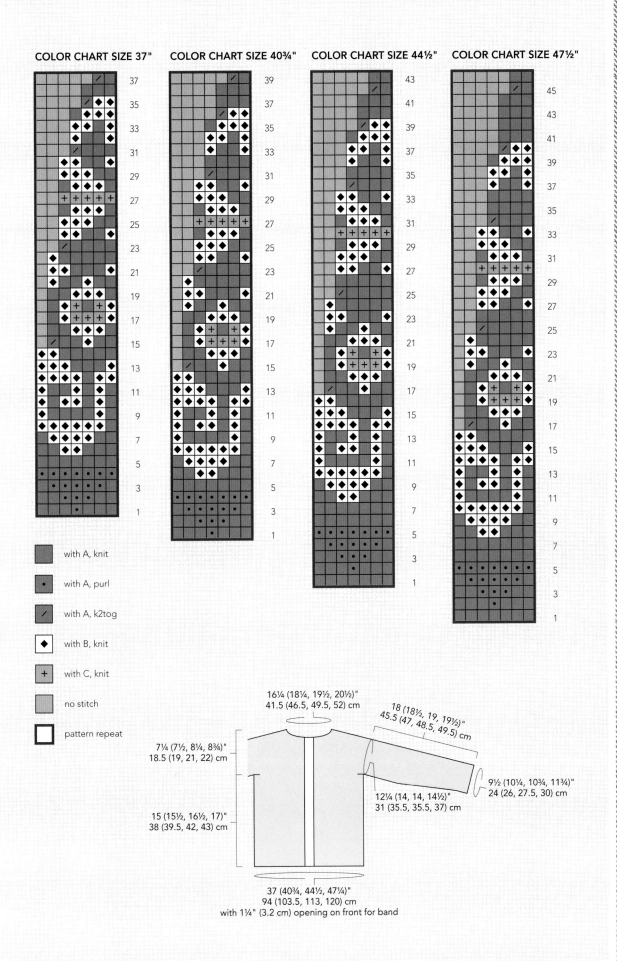

COLOR CHART SIZE 37"

COLOR CHART SIZE 40¾"

COLOR CHART SIZE 44½"

COLOR CHART SIZE 47½"

with A, knit

with A, purl

with A, k2tog

with B, knit

with C, knit

no stitch

pattern repeat

16¼ (18¼, 19½, 20½)"
41.5 (46.5, 49.5, 52) cm

18 (18½, 19, 19½)"
45.5 (47, 48.5, 49.5) cm

7¼ (7½, 8¼, 8¾)"
18.5 (19, 21, 22) cm

9½ (10¼, 10¾, 11¾)"
24 (26, 27.5, 30) cm

12¼ (14, 14, 14½)"
31 (35.5, 35.5, 37) cm

15 (15½, 16½, 17)"
38 (39.5, 42, 43) cm

37 (40¾, 44½, 47¼)"
94 (103.5, 113, 120) cm
with 1¼" (3.2 cm) opening on front for band

halle yoke cardigan

BODY

Using color A and larger cir needle, CO 162 (178, 194, 206). Place marker (pm) for beg of rnd and join for working in the rnd, being careful not to twist sts. Beg of rnd m is at the left side of body.

EST RIBBING AND STEEK: Work 38 (42, 46, 49) sts in 1x1 rib, pm for steek, k10 for center steek column, pm for steek, work 38 (42, 46, 49) sts in 1x1 rib, pm for side, work in 1x1 rib to end.

Cont working even as est until piece meas 1¼" (3.2 cm) from CO edge.

Work even in St st (knit all sts, every rnd) until piece meas 15 (15½, 16½, 17)" (38 [39.5, 42, 43] cm) from CO edge.

Keep sts on cir needle and set aside. Do not break yarn.

SLEEVES

Using color A and dpn, CO 40 (44, 46, 50) sts, distributing evenly over 3 needles. Pm for beg of rnd and join for working in the rnd, being careful not to twist sts.

Work in 1x1 rib for 1½" (3.8 cm).

Shape Sleeve

Knit 10 (8, 10, 13) rnds.

INC RND: K1, M1L (see Glossary), knit to last st, M1R (see Glossary), k1—2 sts inc'd.

Rep the last 11 (9, 11, 14) rnds 5 (7, 6, 5) more times—52 (60, 60, 62) sts.

Work even in St st until piece meas 18 (18½, 19, 19½)" (45.5 [47, 48.5, 49.5] cm) from CO edge.

NEXT RND: K4, place these sts onto st holder or waste yarn, knit to last 4 sts, place rem 4 sts onto st holder or waste yarn—44 (52, 52, 54) sts rem.

Place rem sts onto a separate st holder or waste yarn.

Work second sleeve the same as the first.

YOKE

JOINING RND: Cont with color A attached to body. Remove beg of rnd m, k82 (90, 98, 104) front sts to 4 sts before side m, place next 8 sts onto st holder or waste yarn removing m, return 44 (52, 52, 54) held sts from one sleeve to empty end of cir and knit across, k68 (76, 84, 90) back sts, place next 8 sts onto st holder or waste yarn removing m, return 44 (52, 52, 54) held sts from second sleeve to empty end of cir and knit across, pm for beg of rnd—234 (266, 282, 298) sts.

Work next rnd for your size as foll:

Size 37" only

Knit 1 rnd.

Size 40¾" only

DEC RND: K1, k2tog, k83, k2tog, k54, k2tog, k73, k2tog, knit to end—262 sts rem.

Size 44½" only

INC RND: K1, M1L, knit to end—283 sts rem.

Size 47¼" only

DEC RND: K1, k2tog, knit to end—297 sts rem.

All Sizes

EST COLOR CHART: Work color chart for your size to steek m, taking note of which st of the chart is worked last, sl m, work steek sts by alternating the colors, sl m, then cont working the color chart to end, beg with the following st of the chart.

Cont working color chart as est until all 37 (39, 43, 46) rnds are completed—74 (82, 88, 92) sts rem.

EST RIBBING: Using color A only, work even in 1x1 rib to steek m, sl m, k10, sl m, work even in 1x1 rib to end.

Work in rib for 1" (2.5 cm).

BO all sts in patt.

FINISHING

Complete steek (see Glossary).

Block to measurements.

Buttonband

Using smaller cir needle, color A, and with RS facing, beg at neck edge of left front, pick up and knit 92 (96, 102, 106) sts evenly along left front.

Knit 10 rows, ending after a RS row.

BO all sts loosely.

Buttonhole Band

Using smaller cir needle, color A, and with RS facing, beg at lower edge of right front, pick up and knit 92 (96, 102, 106) sts evenly along right front.

Knit 4 rows ending after a RS row.

Buttonhole row: (WS) K7 (5, 8, 7), *yo, k2tog, k9 (10, 10, 11); rep from * 6 more times, yo, k2tog, k6 (5, 8, 7) to end.

Knit even 5 rows ending after a RS row.

BO all sts loosely.

Join Underarms

Return 8 held underarm sts and sleeve sts to dpn. Graft them together using Kitchener st (see Glossary).

Using needle and button thread, sew buttons onto band so that they line up with buttonholes.

Using tapestry needle, weave in all ends neatly.

Block again if desired.

DART *shawl*

I'm not one of those shawl knitters who love getting lost in a sea of lace and steadily increasing stitch counts. The shawls I mostly knit and wear are workhorses in heavier yarns with tons of texture. This lovely shawl is worked from a wide end to a point, incorporating basic increases and decreases to form an unusual, very wearable arrow shape. The wide end features simple knit-and-purl texture before moving on to the body where a seed-stitch texture highlights the shaping.

finished size

BASE WIDTH: About 43¾" (111 cm).

TOP WIDTH: About 13¾" (35 cm).

LENGTH: About 52" (132 cm).

yarn

Worsted (#4 Medium).

SHOWN HERE: Madelinetosh Tosh Vintage (100% superwash merino wool; 200 yd [182 m]/1½ oz [100 g]): winter wheat, 7 hanks.

needles

Size U.S. 7 (4.5 mm): 32" (80 cm) circular (cir).

Adjust needle size if necessary to obtain the correct gauge.

notions

Markers (m); tapestry needle.

gauge

20½ sts and 32 rows = 4" (10 cm) in body patt.

19 sts and 38 rows = 4" in Zigzag Brocade chart.

note

❋ Circular needle is used to accommodate large number of sts. Do not join; work back and forth in rows.

stitch guide

Body Pattern for Gauge Swatch
(multiple of 2 sts)

ROW 1: (RS) *K1, p1; rep from *.

ROW 2: Purl.

ROW 3: Knit.

ROW 4: Purl.

Rep Rows 1–4 for patt.

Estonian Lateral Braid
(worked over any number of sts)

With left needle tip, lift the strand between the last knitted st and the first st on the left needle (from front to back), knit-tbl of the second stitch on left needle leaving st on needle, knit into first st on left needle, dropping both sts from left needle, *slip 1 st from right needle back to left needle, knit-tbl of the second stitch on left needle leaving st on needle, knit into first st on left needle, dropping both sts from left needle; rep from * to indicated st, then pass second st on right needle over the first.

ZIGZAG BROCADE CHART

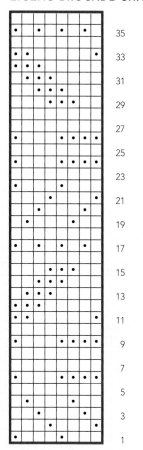

ROMAN STRIPE CHART

	knit on RS; purl on WS
$\cdot$	purl on RS; knit on WS
O	yo
/	k2tog on RS
⁄	k2tog on WS
▨	no stitch
☐	pattern repeat

BASE

CO 208 sts. Do not join; work back and forth in rows.

Knit 1 WS row.

Work Rows 1–36 of Zigzag Brocade chart, then rep Rows 1–16 once more.

Work Rows 1–6 of Roman Stripe chart.

INC ROW: (RS) K104, place marker (pm), M1 (see Glossary), pm, knit to end—209 sts.

NEXT ROW: (WS) K3, purl to last 3 sts, k3.

BODY

ROW 1: K3, k2tog-tbl, knit to m, M1R (see Glossary), sl m, k1, slm, M1L (see Glossary), knit to last 5 sts, k2tog, k3.

ROWS 2 AND 4: (WS) K3, purl to last 3 sts, k3.

ROW 3: K3, k2tog-tbl, [yo, k1, pass yo over knit st] to m, sl m, k1, sl m, [yo, k1, pass yo over knit st] to last 5 sts, k2tog, k3—207 sts rem.

ROW 5: (RS) K3, k2tog-tbl, work Estonian Lateral Braid to m, pass second st on right needle over first st, sl m, k1, sl m, work Estonian Lateral Braid to last 5 sts, pass second st on right needle over first st, k2tog, k3—205 sts rem.

ROW 6: Rep Row 2.

Shape Body

DEC ROW 1: (RS) K3, k2tog-tbl, [k1, p1] to 1 st before m, k1, sl m, k1, sl m, k1, [p1, k1] to last 5 sts, k2tog, k3—2 sts dec'd.

ROWS 2, 4, AND 6: (WS) K3, purl to last 3 sts, k3.

ROW 3: K3, k2tog-tbl, knit to m, M1R, sl m, k1, sl m, M1L, knit to last 3 sts, k2tog, k3.

DEC ROW 5: K3, k2tog-tbl, [k1, p1] to m, sl m, k1, sl m, [p1, k1] to last 5 sts, k2tog, k3—2 sts dec'd.

ROW 7: Rep Row 3.

ROW 8: Rep Row 2.

Rep the last 8 rows 23 times—109 sts rem.

Shape Point

ROW 1: (RS) K3, k2tog-tbl, knit to m, M1R, sl m, k1, sl m, M1L, knit to last 5 sts, k2tog, k3.

ROW 2: (WS) K3, purl to last 3 sts, k3.

DEC ROW 3: K3, k2tog-tbl, knit to last 5 sts, k2tog, k3—2 sts dec'd.

ROW 4: Rep Row 2.

Rep last 4 rows 16 times, then work Rows 1–3 once more—73 sts rem.

Knit 1 WS row, removing markers.

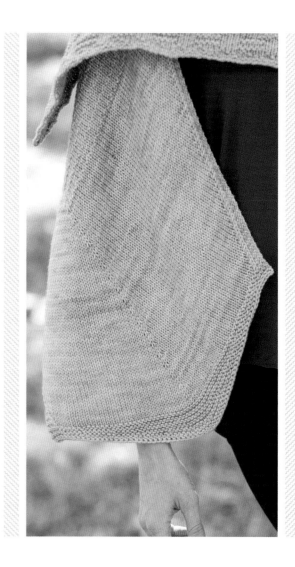

SHORT-ROW 1: (RS) K63, turn so WS is facing; (WS) sl 1 st purlwise with yarn in back (pwise wyb), k52, turn so RS is facing. (See no-wrap short-rows in Glossary.)

SHORT-ROW 2: Sl 1 st pwise wyb, k47, turn so WS is facing; sl 1 st pwise wyb, k42, turn so RS is facing.

SHORT-ROW 3: Sl 1 st pwise wyb, k35, turn so WS is facing; sl 1 st pwise wyb, k28, turn so RS is facing.

SHORT-ROW 4: Sl 1 st pwise wyb, k23, turn so WS is facing; sl 1 st pwise wyb, k18 turn so RS is facing.

SHORT-ROW 5: Sl 1 st pwise wyb, k11, turn so WS is facing; sl 1 st pwise wyb, k4, turn so RS is facing.

NEXT ROW: (RS) Sl 1 st pwise wyb, knit to end closing gaps as you come to them.

NEXT ROW: (WS) Knit to end closing rem gaps as you come to them.

DEC ROW: (RS) K3, k2tog-tbl, knit to last 5 sts, k2tog, k3—71 sts rem.

Knit 1 WS row.

BO all sts loosely kwise.

FINISHING

Using tapestry needle, weave in all ends neatly. Block gently by soaking in lukewarm water until saturated, gently squeeze out much of the water (do not wring), and lay flat on a clean, dry towel or mesh drying rack until completely dry. Shape using pins or blocking wires as needed.

LITTLE ONE *yoke cardigan*

A heavy cardigan with ample ease for layering is a must-have piece. The yarn I've selected for this child's cardigan is a soft, warm blend of wool and alpaca making it more insulating than wool alone. This is a great piece for boys and girls alike—and it's the perfect opportunity to incorporate colors that will speak to the child's personality. This cardigan is worked in the round from the bottom up with steeks; sleeves are knit separately and joined to the body to complete the yoke.

finished size

CHEST CIRCUMFERENCE: About 26¼ (28¼, 29¼, 31½, 35, 36¾)" (66.5 [72, 74.5, 80, 89, 93.5] cm) buttoned with 1¼" (3.2 cm) overlapping buttonband.

TO FIT: 2T (4T, 6y, 8y, 10y, 12y).

Sweater shown measures 29¼" (74.5 cm).

yarn

Aran (#4 Medium).

SHOWN HERE: Artesano Aran (50% alpaca, 50% Highland wool; 144 yd [132 m]/1½ oz [100 g]): #C854 birch (A), 3 (4, 5, 6, 7, 7) hanks; #C850 mahogany (B), 1 hank; #C810 ochre (C), 1 hank.

needles

BODY, SLEEVES, AND YOKE: Size U.S. 8 (5 mm): 16" (40 cm) and 32" (80 cm) circular (cir) and set of 4 double-pointed (dpn).

BUTTONBAND: Size U.S. 7 (4.5 mm): straight.

Adjust needle size if necessary to obtain the correct gauge.

notions

Markers (m); stitch holders or waste yarn; tapestry needle; six 1" (2.5 cm) buttons; needle and button thread for sewing on buttons.

BUTTONS SHOWN HERE: The Durango Button Co., H43/25 Horn Incised (1" [2.5 cm]), 3; Dill Buttons of America, 280733 (1" [2.5 cm]), 3.

gauge

18 sts and 22 rnds = 4" (10 cm) in St st, worked in rnds.

notes

* It is recommended to use a contrasting color stitch marker for the steek markers, to easily tell them apart from other markers used.

* Some of the stitches charted are to be purled rather than knit. This adds texture and visual interest to the color section.

* When working the color chart, work to steek sts, taking note of which st of the chart was worked last, work steek sts by alternating the colors, then cont working the color chart beg with the following st.

stitch guide

1×1 Rib *(multiple of 2 sts)*

RND 1: *K1, p1 rep from * to end.

Rep Rnd 1 for patt.

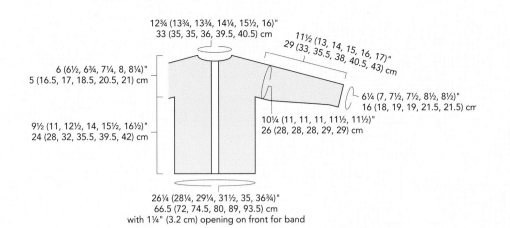

12¾ (13¾, 13¾, 14¼, 15½, 16)"
33 (35, 35, 36, 39.5, 40.5) cm

11½ (13, 14, 15, 16, 17)"
29 (33, 35.5, 38, 40.5, 43) cm

6 (6½, 6¾, 7¼, 8, 8¼)"
5 (16.5, 17, 18.5, 20.5, 21) cm

6¼ (7, 7½, 7½, 8½, 8½)"
16 (18, 19, 19, 21.5, 21.5) cm

9½ (11, 12½, 14, 15½, 16½)"
24 (28, 32, 35.5, 39.5, 42) cm

10¼ (11, 11, 11, 11½, 11½)"
26 (28, 28, 28, 29, 29) cm

26¼ (28¼, 29¼, 31½, 35, 36¾)"
66.5 (72, 74.5, 80, 89, 93.5) cm
with 1¼" (3.2 cm) opening on front for band

little one yoke cardigan

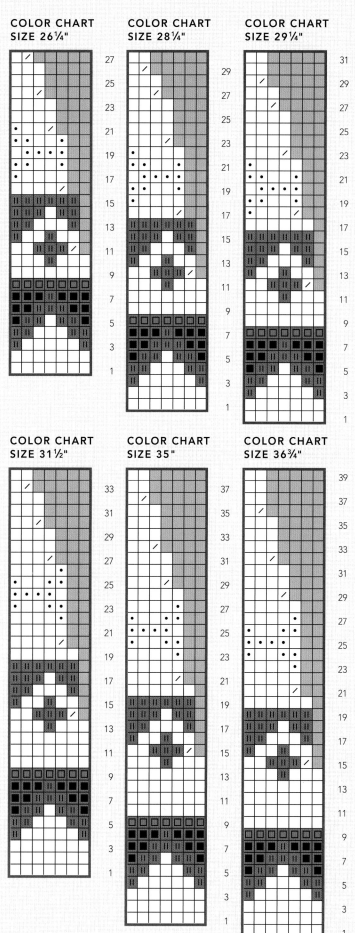

COLOR CHART SIZE 26¼"

COLOR CHART SIZE 28¼"

COLOR CHART SIZE 29¼"

COLOR CHART SIZE 31½"

COLOR CHART SIZE 35"

COLOR CHART SIZE 36¾"

☐	with color A, knit
●	with color A, purl
╱	with color A, k2tog
▦	with color B, knit
▢	with color C, knit
■	with color C, purl
▨	no stitch
☐	pattern repeat

FAMILY-FRIENDLY KNITS

BODY

Using color A and shorter cir needle, CO 124 (134, 138, 148, 164, 172). Place marker (pm) for beg of rnd, and join to work in the rnd, being careful not to twist sts. Beg of rnd m is at the left side of body.

EST RIBBING AND STEEK: P0 (1, 0, 0, 0, 0), k0 (2, 0, 2, 2, 0), [p2, k2] 7 (7, 8, 8, 9, 10) times, pm for steek, k12 for center steek column, pm for steek, k0 (2, 2, 0, 0, 0), [p2, k2] 21 (22, 23, 25, 28, 30) times, p0 (1, 0, 2, 2, 0) to end.

Cont working even as est until piece meas 1¼" (3.2 cm) from CO edge.

Work even in St st (knit all sts, every rnd) until piece meas 9½ (11, 12½, 14, 15½, 16½)" (24 [28, 31.5, 35.5, 39.5, 42] cm) from CO edge.

Keep sts on cir needle and set aside. Do not break yarn.

SLEEVES

Using color A and dpn, CO 28 (32, 34, 34, 38, 38) sts, distributing evenly over 3 needles. Pm for beg of rnd and join for working in the rnd, being careful not to twist sts.

Work in 1x1 rib until piece meas ¾ (¾, 1¼, 1¼, 1¾, 1¾)" (2 [2, 3.2, 3.2, 4.5, 4.5] cm) from CO edge.

Shape Sleeve

INC RND: K1, M1L (see Glossary), knit to last st, M1R (see Glossary), k1—2 sts inc'd.

Knit 4 (5, 6, 7, 8, 9) rnds.

Rep the last 5 (6, 7, 8, 9, 10) rnds 8 (8, 7, 7, 6, 6) more times—46 (50, 50, 50, 52, 52) sts.

Work even in St st until piece meas 11½ (13, 14, 15, 16, 17)" (29 [33, 35.5, 38, 40.5, 43] cm) from CO edge.

NEXT RND: K3 (3, 4, 4, 4, 4), place these sts onto st holder or waste yarn, knit to last 3 (3, 4, 4, 4, 4) sts, place rem 3 (3, 4, 4, 4, 4) sts onto st holder or waste yarn—40 (44, 42, 42, 44, 44) sts rem.

Place rem sts onto a separate st holder or waste yarn.

Work second sleeve the same as the first.

YOKE

JOINING RND: Cont with longer cir and color A attached to body. Remove beg of rnd m, k65 (71, 72, 76, 84, 88) body sts for front, place next 6 (6, 8, 8, 8, 8) sts onto st holder or waste yarn, return 40 (44, 42, 42, 44, 44) held sts from one sleeve to empty end of cir and knit across, k50 (54, 54, 60, 68, 72) body sts for back, place next 6 (6, 8, 8, 8, 8) sts onto st holder or waste yarn, return 40 (44, 42, 42, 44, 44) held sts from second sleeve to empty end of cir and knit across, pm for beg of rnd—192 (210, 206, 216, 236, 244) sts.

Work next rnd for your size as foll:

Sizes 26¼ (29¼)″ only

INC RND: K1, M1L, knit to 1 st before sleeve, M1R, knit to end—194 (208) sts.

Size 28¼″ only

DEC RND: K1, k2tog, knit to 1 st before sleeve, ssk, knit to end—208 sts rem.

Sizes 31½ (36¾)″ only

DEC RND: K1, k2tog, knit to end—215 (243) sts rem.

Size 35″ only

Knit 1 rnd.

All Sizes

EST COLOR CHART: Begin color chart for your size to steek m, taking note of which st of the chart is worked last, sl m, work steek sts by alternating the colors, sl m, then cont working the color chart to end, beg with the following st of the chart.

Cont working color chart as est until all 27 (30, 31, 34, 38, 39) rnds are completed, changing to shorter cir needle or dpn when sts no longer fit comfortably on longer cir needle—64 (68, 68, 70, 76, 78) sts rem.

EST RIBBING: Using color A only, work even in 1x1 rib to steek m, sl m, k12, sl m, work even in 1x1 rib to end.

Work in rib for 1" (2.5 cm).

BO all sts in patt.

FINISHING

Complete steek (see Glossary).

Block to measurements.

Buttonband

Using straight needles, color A, and with RS facing, beg at lower edge of right front for a boy (or neck edge of left front for a girl), pick up and knit 64 (73, 80, 88, 97, 102) sts evenly along front edge.

Knit 7 rows, ending after a WS row.

BO all sts loosely.

Buttonhole Band

Using straight needles, color A, and with RS facing, beg at neck edge of left front for a boy (or lower edge of right front for a girl), pick up and knit 64 (73, 80, 88, 97, 102) sts evenly along front edge.

Knit 3 rows, ending after a WS row.

BUTTONHOLE ROW: (RS) K4 (3, 4, 3, 3, 3), *yo, k2tog, k9 (11, 12, 14, 16, 17); rep from * 4 more times, yo, k2tog, k3 (3, 4, 3, 2, 2).

Knit 3 rows, ending after a WS row.

BO all sts loosely.

Join Underarms

Return 6 (6, 8, 8, 8, 8) held sts from body and sleeve to dpn. Join color A and graft them together using Kitchener st (see Glossary).

Using tapestry needle, weave in all ends neatly.

Block again if desired.

CHOOSE-YOUR-OWN-ADVENTURE
cowl ⌘

This project is a lovely introduction to stranded knitting. If you want to make the cowls as shown, just follow the instructions and the charts for the samples. But for those who are feeling a bit more adventurous, I've provided four charts that can be used in various configurations to create completely different patterns. Mix up the colors as well and you'll have infinite possibilities. (You can even use the three charts with the toques on page 84 for even more variations.)

finished size

About 24½" (62 cm) circumference and 7" (18 cm) long; to fit an adult.

yarn

Fingering (#1 Super Fine).

SHOWN HERE: Jamieson's Shetland Spindrift (100% Highland wool; 115 yd [105 m]/25 g):

SAMPLE 1: #293 port wine (A), #435 apricot (B), #768 eggshell (C); 1 ball each color.

SAMPLE 2: #730 dark navy (A), #575 lipstick (B), #329 laurel (C); 1 ball each color.

needles

Size U.S. 4 (3.5 mm): 16" (40 cm) circular (cir).

Adjust needle size if necessary to obtain the correct gauge.

notions

Markers (m); tapestry needle.

gauge

30 sts and 33 rnds = 4" (10 cm) in color charts, worked in rnds.

notes

✳ This pattern is a base for you to work from in designing a beautiful stranded-color cowl. Assign colors A, B, and C of your choosing to colors 1, 2, and 3 in the patterns provided and change color assignments and patterns freely from one row repeat to the next.

✳ If you choose to use only two-color patterns with one color as the main color, you might need two skeins of the main color to complete your cowl.

✳ Charts E, F, and G are on page 87. You can use any of these charts as well.

✳ If you've worked color stranding in the past, you will have learned that twisting the strands behind the work (the floats) is to be avoided. The Latvian braid is designed to twist the yarn in front of the work first in one direction on Rnd 4 of chart B, then untwist the yarn on Rnd 5.

stitch guide

Latvian Braid Right

Bring both color strands of yarn to the front of the work, *with color 1, p1, bring color 3 under color 1; with color 3, p1, bring color 1 under color 3; rep from *.

Latvian Braid Left

Bring both color strands of yarn to the front of the work, *with color 1, p1, bring color 3 over color 1; with color 3, p1, bring color 1 over color 3; rep from *.

2x2 Rib *(multiple of 4 sts)*

RND 1: *K2, p2; rep from *.

Rep Rnd 1 for patt.

COWL SAMPLE 1 CHART **COWL SAMPLE 2 CHART**

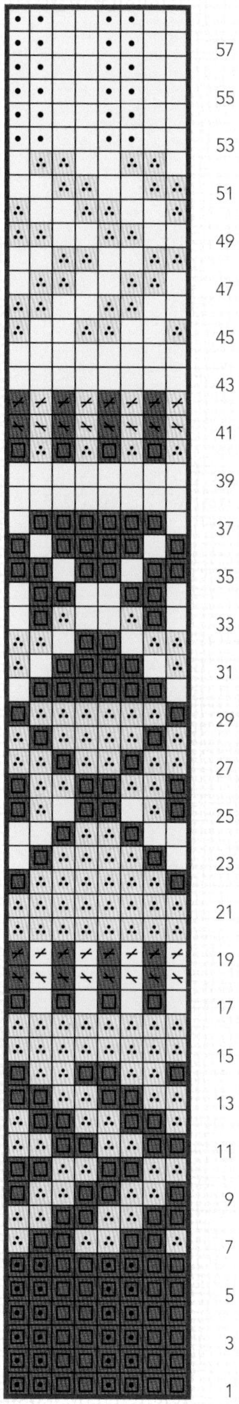

Cowl Sample 1 chart row numbers (right side): 57, 55, 53, 51, 49, 47, 45, 43, 41, 39, 37, 35, 33, 31, 29, 27, 25, 23, 21, 19, 17, 15, 13, 11, 9, 7, 5, 3, 1

Cowl Sample 2 chart row numbers (right side): 57, 55, 53, 51, 49, 47, 45, 43, 41, 39, 37, 35, 33, 31, 29, 27, 25, 23, 21, 19, 17, 15, 13, 11, 9, 7, 5, 3, 1

Legend (top right):
- with color A, knit
- with color A, purl
- with color B, knit
- with color B, purl
- with color C, knit
- with color C, purl
- pattern repeat

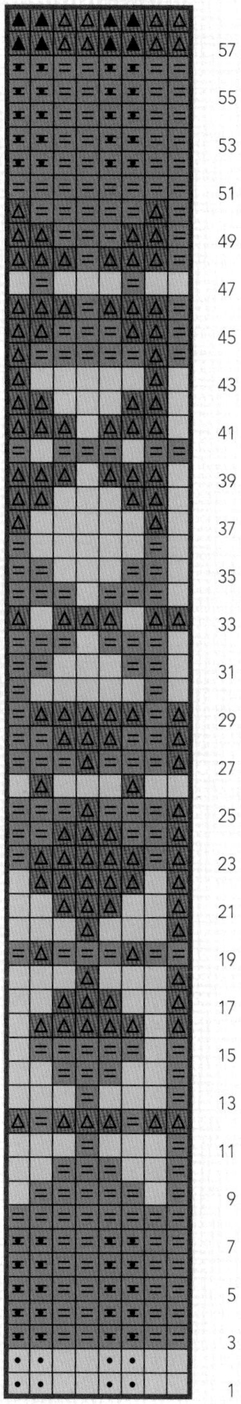

CHART A   **CHART B**

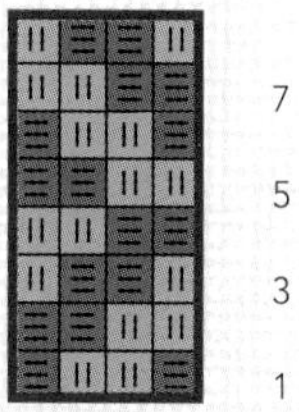

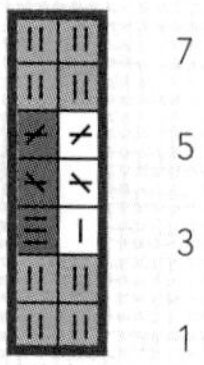

Chart A row numbers: 7, 5, 3, 1
Chart B row numbers: 7, 5, 3, 1

CHART C

Chart C row numbers: 7, 5, 3, 1

CHART D

Chart D row numbers: 7, 5, 3, 1

- I color 1
- II color 2
- = color 3
- Latvian braid right indicated color
- Latvian braid left indicated color
- pattern repeat

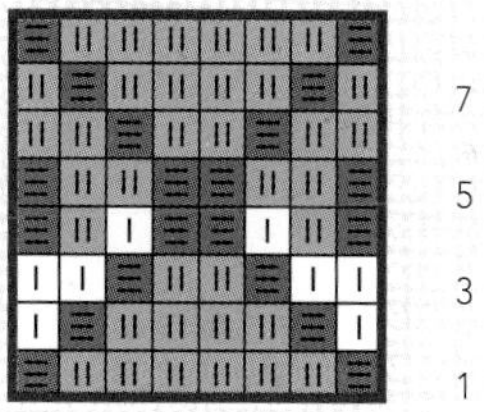

Legend (bottom left):
- with color A, knit
- with color A, purl
- with color B, knit
- with color C, knit
- with color C, purl
- Latvian braid right in indicated color
- Latvian braid left in indicated color
- pattern repeat

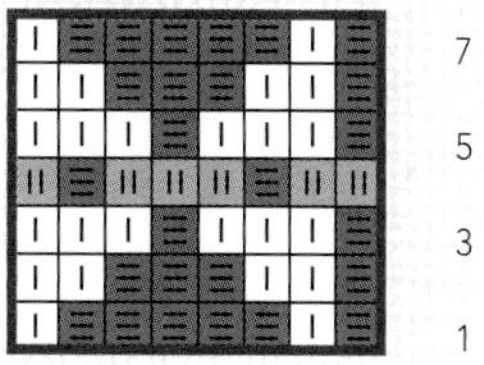

COWL

Using color selected for ribbing, CO 184 sts. Place marker (pm) for beg of rnd and join to work in the rnd, being careful not to twist sts.

Work in 2x2 rib until piece meas ¾" (3.2 cm) or desired length from CO edge. (This is Rnds 1–6 of the sample charts.)

Follow the sample charts using the colors listed under Yarn (page 80) or choose your own charts and 2 or 3 colors and work a total of 6 chart reps.

Work in 2x2 rib for ¾" (3.2 cm) or desired length. (This is Rnds 53–58 of the sample charts.)

BO all sts in patt.

FINISHING

Using tapestry needle, weave in all ends neatly.

Block to measurements.

CHOOSE-YOUR-OWN-ADVENTURE *toque*

With this versatile project, you get to make hats for the whole family. I've designed four toppers—for Mom, Dad, and the kids—but, as with the cowls on page 78, you can mix and match charts and colors to create custom designs. Let your imagination run wild and design strikingly different styles for each special person in your life.

finished size

About 16 (18¼, 19¼, 20¼)" (40.5 [46.5, 49, 51.5] cm) head circumference and 7¼ (7½, 8½, 8½)" (18.5 [19, 21.5, 21.5] cm) long.

TO FIT: Toddler (Child, Adult S, Adult L).

Hats shown measure 18¼", 19¼", and 20¼" (46.5, 49, and 51.5 cm).

yarn

Fingering (#1 Super Fine).

SHOWN HERE: Jamieson's Shetland Spindrift (100% Highland wool; 115 yd [105 m]/25 g):

SAMPLE 1: #820 bottle (A), #764 cloud (B), #1160 scotch broom (C); 1 ball each color.

SAMPLE 2: #423 burnt ochre (A), #235 grouse (B), #603 pot-pourri (C); 1 ball each color.

SAMPLE 3: #688 mermaid (A), #227 earth (B); 1 ball each color.

SAMPLE 4: #868 leather (A), #410 cornfield (B), #423 burnt ochre (C), #293 port wine (D); 1 ball each color.

needles

Size U.S. 4 (3.5 mm): 16" (40 cm) circular (cir) and set of 4 or 5 double-pointed (dpn).

Adjust needle size if necessary to obtain the correct gauge.

notions

Markers (m); tapestry needle.

gauge

30 sts and 33 rnds = 4" (10 cm) in color charts, worked in rnds.

notes

* This pattern is a base for you to work from in designing a beautiful stranded-color toque. Assign colors A, B, and C of your choosing to colors 1, 2, and 3 in the patterns provided and change color assignment and patterns freely from one row repeat to the next.

* If you're knitting a size Adult S or Adult L toque and choose to use only two-color patterns with one color as the main color, you might need two skeins of the main color to complete your toque.

* Charts A, B, and C are on page 81. You can use any of these charts as well.

* If you've worked color stranding in the past, you will have learned that twisting the strands behind the work (the floats) is to be avoided. The Latvian braid is designed to twist the yarn in front of the work first in one direction on Rnds 15, 22, 29, and 36 of the Sample 4 chart, then untwist the yarn on Rnds 16, 23, 30, and 37.

stitch guide

Latvian Braid Right

Bring both color strands of yarn to the front of the work, *with color 1, p1, bring color 3 under color 1; with color 3, p1, bring color 1 under color 3; rep from *.

Latvian Braid Left

Bring both color strands of yarn to the front of the work, *with color 1, p1, bring color 3 over color 1; with color 3, p1, bring color 1 over color 3; rep from *.

2×2 Rib (multiple of 4 sts)

RND 1: *K2, p2; rep from *.

Rep Rnd 1 for patt.

CHART D

7

5

3

1

CHART E

7

5

3

1

CHART F

7

5

3

1

CHART G

7

5

3

1

I	color 1
II	color 2
≡	color 3
☐	pattern repeat

TOQUE SAMPLE 1 CHART

	47
	45
	43
	41
	39
	37
	35
	33
	31
	29
	27
	25
	23
	21
	19
	17
	15
	13
	11
	9
	7
	5
	3
	1

- ▢ with color A, knit
- ■ with color A, purl
- ○ with color B, knit
- ∴ with color C, knit
- ▢ pattern repeat

TOQUE SAMPLE 2 CHART

	47
	45
	43
	41
	39
	37
	35
	33
	31
	29
	27
	25
	23
	21
	19
	17
	15
	13
	11
	9
	7
	5
	3
	1

- ◇ with color A, knit
- ◆ with color A, purl
- ✚ with color B, knit
- ◹ with color C, knit
- ▢ pattern repeat

TOQUE SAMPLE 3 CHART

	39
	37
	35
	33
	31
	29
	27
	25
	23
	21
	19
	17
	15
	13
	11
	9
	7
	5
	3
	1

- ◿ with color A, knit
- ◢ with color A, purl
- ✕ with color B, knit
- ▢ pattern repeat

TOQUE SAMPLE 4 CHART

	39
	37
	35
	33
	31
	29
	27
	25
	23
	21
	19
	17
	15
	13
	11
	9
	7
	5
	3
	1

- ○ with color A, knit
- ● with color A, purl
- — with color B, knit
- ◇ with color C, knit
- ▣ with color D, knit
- ✔ Latvian braid right in indicated c
- ✘ Latvian braid left in indicated co
- ▢ pattern repeat

TOQUE

Using color selected for ribbing and cir needle, CO 120 (136, 144, 152) sts. Place marker (pm) for beg of rnd and join to work in the rnd, being careful not to twist sts.

Work in 2x2 rib until piece meas 1¼" (3.2 cm) or desired length from CO edge. (This is Rnds 1–12 in the charts for Samples 1 and 2 and Rnds 1–13 in the charts for Samples 3 and 4.)

Follow the sample charts using the colors listed under Yarn (page 86) or choose your own charts and 2 or 3 colors and work a total of 4 (4, 5, 5) reps before moving on to crown shaping.

Shape Crown

note: Change to dpn when sts no longer fit comfortably on cir needle.

SET-UP RND: Using color selected for crown, *k13 (15, 16, 17), k2tog, pm; rep from *—112 (128, 136, 144) sts rem.

NEXT RND: Knit.

DEC RND: Knit to 2 sts before m, k2tog, sl m; rep from *—8 sts dec'd.

Rep the last 2 rnds 8 more times—40 (56, 64, 72) sts.

Rep dec rnd every rnd 3 (5, 6, 7) times—16 sts rem.

NEXT RND: *K2tog, remove m; rep from *—8 sts rem.

FINISHING

Break yarn, leaving 3" (7.5 cm) tail and use tapestry needle to thread through rem sts. Gently pull sts closed, weave in ends, and block well (see Blocking on page 90). Attach optional pom-pom (see Glossary) at center of crown closure.

BLOCKING

Blocking neatly is as important to your knitted piece as your gauge. Hats are especially awkward to block, and knitters—being the clever people we are—have come up with many ways to get the job done, from blowing up balloons as blockers for beanies to using plates for shaping berets nicely. For these toques, I have blocked them with both round and flat crowns; this is how it's done:

you will need

¼" (6 mm) or ½" (1.3 cm) dowel (available in packs precut to about 18" [45.5 cm])

19" (48.5 cm) diameter foam ball from the craft store (the really hard foam will shed little fragments everywhere and need to be covered with fabric; on the upside, it's actually much easier to use than the pressed Styrofoam ones for this purpose)

Medium-size floral foam block

5½" (14 cm) or 6" (15 cm) embroidery hoop (for flat crown)

STEP 1: Jab the dowel into the foam ball and cover with fabric if you're using the hard foam.

STEP 2: Jab the dowel with foam ball in place into the center of the floral foam block.

STEP 3 (flat crown only): Remove the inner ring of the embroidery hoop and place it on top of the foam ball like a crown.

STEP 4: Gently pull the hat over the foam ball, centering it over the hoop (for flat crown).

You want the hat to drape nice and straight without bunching at the bottom. Leave it to air-dry and you'll be amazed at how beautifully blocked it is!

NATIVE *poncho*

Ponchos are typically rectangles seamed together or worked as a sweater without sleeves, but I wanted to create something new that was seamless, packed with texture, and engaging to knit. This unusual shaping was inspired by the two-needle cast-on (see Glossary), which allows the fabric to grow from the center back to the front hemline. Though the cast-on method may take some practice, this project will be an enjoyable knit for all experience levels.

finished size

WIDTH: About 23½ (25¼, 27, 28¾)" (59.5 [64, 68.5, 73] cm).

LENGTH: About 20¼ (23, 26¼, 26¾)" (51.5 [58.5, 66.5, 68] cm).

To fit 32/34 (36/38, 40/44, 46/48)" (81.5–86.5 [91.5–96.5, 101.5–106.5, 117–122] cm) bust circumference.

Poncho shown measures 25¼" (64 cm).

yarn

Worsted (#4 Medium).

SHOWN HERE: Quince and Co. Owl Tweet (100% alpaca; 120 yd [110 m]/3/4 oz [50 g]): #368 boysenberry, 7 (8, 10, 10) skeins.

needles

Size U.S. 6 (4 mm): 32" (80 cm) circular (cir).

Adjust needle size if necessary to obtain the correct gauge.

notions

Marker (m); stitch holders or waste yarn; tapestry needle.

gauge

19 sts and 28 rows = 4" (10 cm) in Arrow Stripe charts.

notes

- This poncho is cast on at the center back using a two-needle cast-on (see Glossary) that may take a couple of attempts before you feel comfortable working. I suggest casting on a swatch size to get into the rhythm before diving into the large number of stitches the poncho requires.

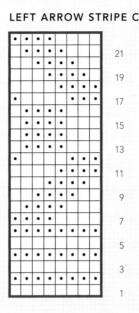

LEFT ARROW STRIPE CHART

RIGHT ARROW STRIPE CHART

	knit on RS; purl on WS
•	purl on RS; knit on WS
	pattern repeat

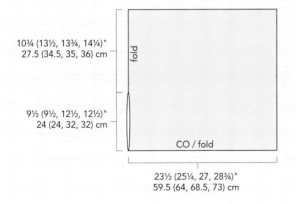

10¾ (13½, 13¾, 14¼)"
27.5 (34.5, 35, 36) cm

fold

9½ (9½, 12½, 12½)"
24 (24, 32, 32) cm

CO / fold

23½ (25¼, 27, 28¾)"
59.5 (64, 68.5, 73) cm

native poncho

RIGHT BACK

Using two-needle cast-on (see Glossary), CO 112 (120, 128, 136) sts on each end of cir needle, placing a marker between them.

ROW 1: Work Row 1 of Right Arrow Stripe chart to m, remove m and place rem 112 (120, 128, 136) sts onto st holder or waste yarn for left back.

Cont working Right Arrow Stripe chart until Rows 1–22 are completed 3 (3, 4, 4) times. Break yarn and place sts onto st holder or waste yarn.

LEFT BACK

Return 112 (120, 128, 136) held left back sts to needle and join yarn preparing to work a RS row.

Work Rows 1–22 of Left Arrow Stripe chart 3 (3, 4, 4) times.

FRONT

Work Row 1 of Left Arrow Stripe chart to end of left back sts, pm, return 112 (120, 128, 136) held right back sts to empty end of needle and work Row 1 of Right Arrow Stripe chart to end—224 (240, 256, 272) sts.

Cont working Arrow Stripe charts as est until Rows 1–22 are completed 3 (4, 4, 4) more times, then rep Rows 1–7 (1–6, 1–5, 1–8) once more.

Knit 3 (0, 3, 3) rows.

BO all sts loosely.

FINISHING

Using tapestry needle, weave in all ends neatly.

Block to measurements.

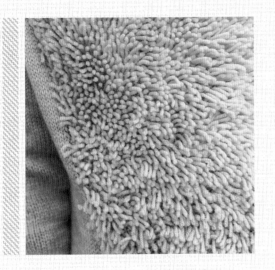

A LITTLE WILD
raglan pullover ⌘

This charming pullover is the perfect way to capture your child's wild nature. Our wild child is a lioness, protective and fierce. Maybe your little one is more of a lamb—choose warm gray or cream and leave the loop stitch uncut. Does he climb the walls like a monkey or squeeze you like a bear? Go for rich, heather browns. Maybe she's a nature lover, rolling around in the grass and helping in the garden—choose a bright, grassy green. You know your little beast best.

finished size

About 23¼ (26¼, 28¾, 31¼, 33¼)" (59 [66.5, 73, 79.5, 84.5] cm) chest circumference.

TO FIT: 2T (4T, 6y, 8y, 10y).

Pullover shown measures 28¾" (73 cm).

yarn

DK (#3 Light).

SHOWN HERE: Cephalopod Yarns Traveller (100% superwash merino wool; 280 yd [256 m]/114 g): #C12 grand palais, 2 (3, 3, 4, 4) skeins.

needles

Size U.S. 6 (4 mm): 16" (40 cm) and 24" (60 cm) circular (cir) and set of 4 or 5 double-pointed (dpn).

Adjust needle size if necessary to obtain the correct gauge.

notions

Markers (m); stitch holders or waste yarn; tapestry needle; blocking wire (optional).

gauge

24 sts and 31 rnds = 4" (10 cm) in St st, worked in rnds.

16 sts and 29 rnds = 4" (10 cm) in Loop st, worked in rnds.

notes

✳ This raglan sweater is knit in the round from the top down, and the loop stitch is worked between stitch markers from the edge of the collar to ¾" (2 cm) before the hem ribbing. The loop stitch will cause a minor slant or warp in the knitting, which is straightened by using blocking wires and pins in finishing. You can leave loops intact or cut them as pictured.

✳ It is recommended to use a contrasting color stitch marker for the beg of rnd and loop st markers, to easily tell them apart from other markers used.

stitch guide

1×1 Rib *(multiple of 2 sts)*

RND 1: *K1, p1; rep from *.

Rep Rnd 1 for patt.

Loop Stitch *(multiple of 2 sts)*

RND 1: *K1, leave st on left needle, bring yarn forward between needles, wrap around left thumb to create loop about 1" (2.5 cm), bring yarn back between needles, knit st on left needle again, slip off needle, yo, pass 2 knit sts over yo; rep from *.

RND 2: Knit.

Rep Rnds 1 and 2 for patt.

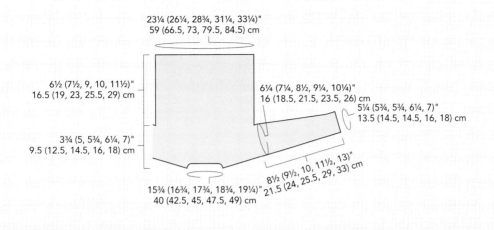

23¼ (26¼, 28¾, 31¼, 33¼)"
59 (66.5, 73, 79.5, 84.5) cm

6½ (7½, 9, 10, 11½)"
16.5 (19, 23, 25.5, 29) cm

6¼ (7¼, 8½, 9¼, 10¼)"
16 (18.5, 21.5, 23.5, 26) cm

5¼ (5¾, 5¾, 6¼, 7)"
13.5 (14.5, 14.5, 16, 18) cm

3¾ (5, 5¾, 6¼, 7)"
9.5 (12.5, 14.5, 16, 18) cm

8½ (9½, 10, 11½, 13)"
21.5 (24, 25.5, 29, 33) cm

15¾ (16¾, 17¾, 18¾, 19¼)"
40 (42.5, 45, 47.5, 49) cm

a little wild raglan pullover

YOKE

Using shorter cir needle or dpn, CO 78 (84, 88, 94, 96) sts. Place marker (pm) for beg of rnd and join to work in the rnd, being careful not to twist sts.

Work in 1x1 rib until piece meas 1" (2.5 cm) from CO edge.

Shape Raglan

note: *Change to longer cir needle when sts no longer fit comfortably on shorter cir or dpn.*

SET-UP RND: K30 (32, 32, 36, 36) for back, pm for raglan, k7 (8, 9, 9, 10) for sleeve, pm for raglan, k1, pm for loop patt, k32 (34, 36, 38, 38), pm for Loop st, k1, pm for raglan, k7 (8, 9, 9, 10) for front.

INC AND EST LOOP ST: [K1, M1L (see Glossary), knit to 1 st before raglan m, M1R (see Glossary), k1, sl m] twice, k1, M1L, sl m, work in Loop st to next m, sl m, M1R, k1, sl m, k1, M1L, knit to last st, M1R, k1—86 (92, 96, 102, 104) sts; 9 (10, 11, 11, 12) sts each sleeve, 32 (34, 34, 38, 38) sts for back and 36 (38, 40, 42, 42) sts for front.

Work 1 rnd even as est, working inc'd sts into St st (knit all sts, every rnd) as they appear.

INC RND: *K1, M1L, work as est to 1 st before m, M1R, k1, sl m; rep from * 3 more times—8 sts inc'd.

Rep last 2 rnds 11 (14, 17, 19, 22) more times—182 (212, 240, 262, 288) sts; 33 (40, 47, 51, 58) sts each sleeve, 56 (64, 70, 78, 84) sts for back and 60 (68, 76, 82, 88) sts for front.

Divide Body and Sleeves

Using shorter cir needle, k56 (64, 70, 78, 84) back sts to m, remove m, place next 33 (40, 47, 51, 58) sts onto st holder or waste yarn for sleeve, remove m, use the backward-loop method (see Glossary) to CO 4 sts, work 60 (68, 76, 82, 88) front sts as est, remove m, place next 33 (40, 47, 51, 58) sts onto st holder or waste yarn for sleeve, remove m, use the backward-loop method to CO 2 sts, pm for beg of rnd, then CO 2 more sts, and join to work in the rnds—124 (140, 154, 168, 180) sts.

BODY

Work even in St st until piece meas 4 (5, 6½, 7½, 9)" (10 [12.5, 16.5, 19, 23] cm) from divide, ending after Rnd 2 of Loop st.

Work all sts in St st for ¾" (2 cm).

Work in 1x1 rib for 1¾" (4.5 cm).

BO all sts in patt.

SLEEVES

Return 33 (40, 47, 51, 58) held sts from 1 sleeve to dpn, and knit across, pick up and knit 2 sts at underarm, pm for beg of rnd, then pick up and knit 2 more sts and join to work in the rnd—37 (44, 51, 55, 62) sts.

Knit 1 (2, 1, 1, 2) rnd(s).

Sizes 23¼ (28¾, 31¼)" only

DEC RND: K1, k2tog, knit to end—36 (50, 54) sts.

Shape Sleeve

All Sizes

Knit 23 (10, 7, 8, 7) rnds.

DEC RND: K1, k2tog, knit to last 3 sts, ssk, k1—2 sts dec'd.

Rep the last 24 (11, 8, 9, 8) rnds 1 (3, 7, 4, 3) more time(s)—32 (36, 34, 44, 54) sts rem.

[Knit 0 (11, 0, 9, 8) rnds, then rep dec rnd] 0 (1, 0, 3, 6) time(s)—32 (34, 34, 38, 42) sts rem.

Cont to work even in St st until piece meas 7¼ (8¼, 8¾, 10¼, 11¾)" (18.5 [21, 22, 26, 30] cm) from divide.

Work in 1x1 rib for 1¼" (3.2 cm).

BO all sts in patt.

Work second sleeve the same as the first.

FINISHING

Using tapestry needle, weave in all ends neatly. Block to measurements.

note: *To straighten the loop-stitch panel, thread blocking wires up the right and left sides of the panel and pin in place making sure the wires are nicely parallel and the piece is smoothed flat.*

PEAK *tank* ⌘

This soft, comfortable top is the ultimate layering piece for cooler weather. Subtle details make this tank special and enjoyable to knit. With relaxing stitches, a simple construction, and a deceptively simple lace panel, this is a top that's as much fun to make as it is to wear.

finished size

About 43 (45¼, 47½, 50, 52¼, 55¾, 58¼)" (109 [115, 120.5, 127, 132.5, 141.5, 148] cm) bust circumference.

Pullover shown measures 45¼" (115 cm).

yarn

DK (#3 Light).

SHOWN HERE: Manos Del Uruguay Serena (60% baby alpaca, 40% pima cotton; 170 yd [155 m]/3/4 oz [50 g]): #2150 fig, 4 (4, 5, 5, 5, 5, 6) skeins.

needles

Size U.S. 5 (3.75 mm): 16" (40 cm) and 32" (80 cm) circular (cir) and set of 4 or 5 double-pointed (dpn).

Adjust needle size if necessary to obtain the correct gauge.

notions

Markers (m); stitch holders or waste yarn; tapestry needle.

gauge

27 sts and 33 rnds = 4" (10 cm) in St st, worked in rnds.

notes

- This warm-weather pullover is knit in the round from the bottom up with simple shaping in the front to form a subtle point. The front and back are separated and worked in three pieces. The front left and right are then grafted to the back left and right before finishing armholes and neck in simple stockinette.
- It is recommended to use a contrasting color stitch marker for the beg of rnd and center front markers, to easily tell them apart from other markers used.

PEAK CHART

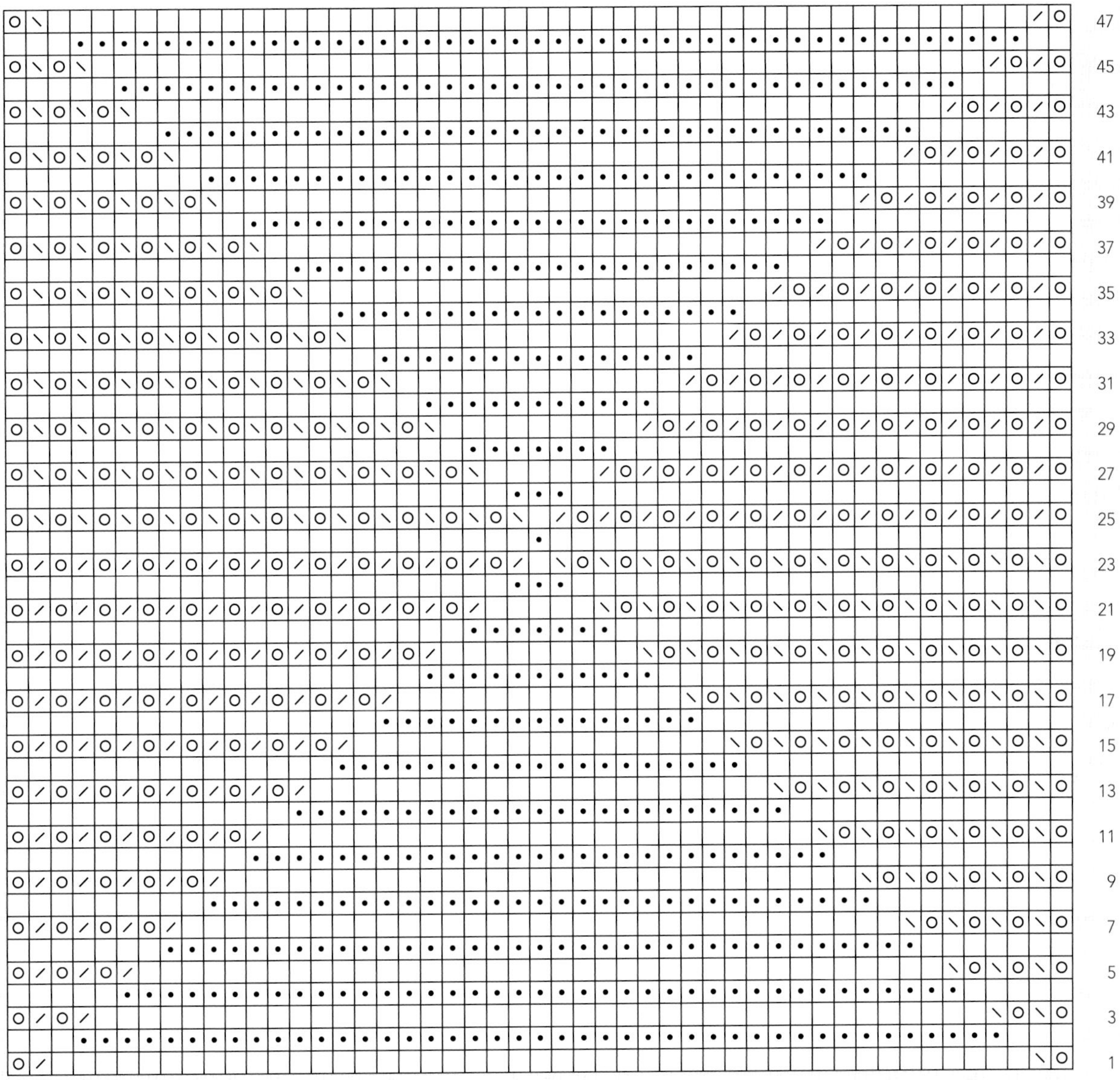

Chart with rows numbered 1 through 47 (odd numbers labeled on the right side: 1, 3, 5, 7, 9, 11, 13, 15, 17, 19, 21, 23, 25, 27, 29, 31, 33, 35, 37, 39, 41, 43, 45, 47).

Legend:

(empty box)	knit on RS; purl on WS
•	purl on RS; knit on WS
O	yo
∕	k2tog
∖	ssk

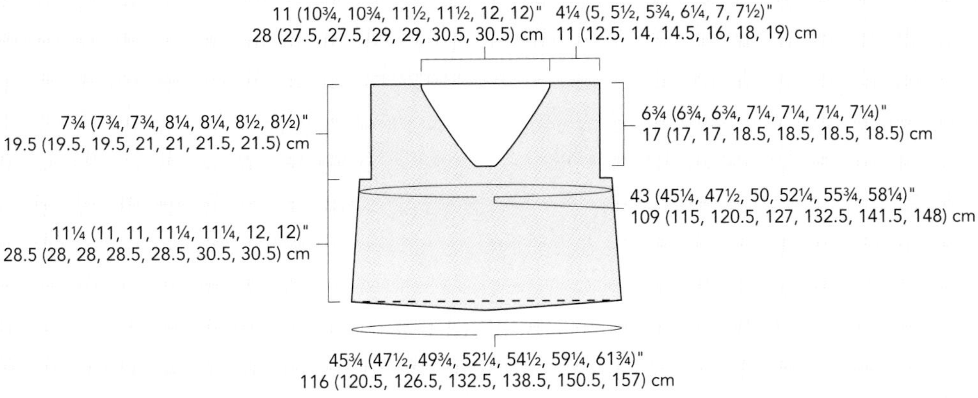

11 (10¾, 10¾, 11½, 11½, 12, 12)"
28 (27.5, 27.5, 29, 29, 30.5, 30.5) cm   4¼ (5, 5½, 5¾, 6¼, 7, 7½)"
11 (12.5, 14, 14.5, 16, 18, 19) cm

7¾ (7¾, 7¾, 8¼, 8¼, 8½, 8½)"
19.5 (19.5, 19.5, 21, 21, 21.5, 21.5) cm

6¾ (6¾, 6¾, 7¼, 7¼, 7¼, 7¼)"
17 (17, 17, 18.5, 18.5, 18.5, 18.5) cm

43 (45¼, 47½, 50, 52¼, 55¾, 58¼)"
109 (115, 120.5, 127, 132.5, 141.5, 148) cm

11¼ (11, 11, 11¼, 11¼, 12, 12)"
28.5 (28, 28, 28.5, 28.5, 30.5, 30.5) cm

45¾ (47½, 49¾, 52¼, 54½, 59¼, 61¾)"
116 (120.5, 126.5, 132.5, 138.5, 150.5, 157) cm

BODY

Using longer cir needle, CO 308 (320, 336, 352, 368, 400, 416) sts. Place marker (pm) for beg of rnd and join to work in the rnd, being careful not to twist sts.

Knit 5 rnds.

Purl 1 rnd.

Shape Front

SET-UP RND: K77 (80, 84, 88, 92, 100, 104), pm for center front, M1 (see Glossary), pm for center front, k77 (80, 84, 88, 92, 100, 104), pm for side, k154 (160, 168, 176, 184, 200, 208) to end for back—309 (321, 337, 353, 369, 401, 417) sts.

Knit 8 (9, 9, 9, 9, 6, 6) rnds.

DEC RND: Knit to 2 sts before center front m, ssk, sl m, k1, sl m, k2tog, knit to end—2 sts dec'd.

Rep the last 9 (10, 10, 10, 10, 7, 7) rnds 4 (3, 3, 2, 2, 4, 4) more times—299 (313, 329, 347, 363, 391, 407) sts rem; 145 (153, 161, 171, 179, 191, 199) sts for front and 154 (160, 168, 176, 184, 200, 208) sts for back.

[Knit 9 (10, 10, 10, 10, 7, 7) rnds, then rep dec rnd] 4 (4, 4, 5, 5, 7, 7) times—291 (305, 321, 337, 353, 377, 393) sts rem; 137 (145, 153, 161, 169, 177, 185) sts for front and 154 (160, 168, 176, 184, 200, 208) sts for back.

Separate Front and Back

NEXT RND: K6, place last 6 sts onto st holder or waste yarn, k125 (133, 141, 149, 157, 165, 173) front sts to 6 sts before side m, k12 removing m, place last 12 sts onto st holder or waste yarn, k142 (148, 156, 164, 172, 188, 196) back to last 6 sts, place next 6 sts onto st holder or waste yarn.

Cont working back and forth on 142 (148, 156, 164, 172, 188, 196) back sts only. Place 125 (133, 141, 149, 157, 165, 173) front sts (including center front markers) onto st holder or waste yarn to be worked later.

BACK

NEXT ROW: (WS) Sl 1 st purlwise with yarn in front (pwise wyf), purl to end.

NEXT ROW: (RS) Sl 1 st pwise with yarn in back (wyb), knit to end.

Rep the last 2 rows 4 (4, 4, 6, 6, 6, 6) more times, then work 1 more WS row.

DEC ROW: (RS) Sl 1 st pwise with yarn in back (wyb), k9 (8, 8, 8, 8, 8, 6), k2tog, *k13 (14, 15, 16, 17, 12, 13), k2tog; rep from * 7 (7, 7, 7, 7, 11, 11) more times, k10 (9, 9, 9, 9, 9, 7)—133 (139, 147, 155, 163, 175, 183) sts rem.

NEXT ROW: (WS) Sl 1 pwise wyf, purl to end.

EST PEAK CHART: (RS) Sl 1 st pwise wyb, work 41 (44, 48, 52, 56, 62, 66) sts in St st (knit on RS, purl on WS), pm, work 49 sts in Peak chart, pm, work 42 (45, 49, 53, 57, 63, 67) sts in St st to end.

Cont working even as est, slipping first st of each row until all 47 rows of Peak chart are completed.

Work 3 (3, 3, 5, 5, 7, 7) rows even in St st, slipping the first st of each row, ending after a WS row.

Place 29 (33, 37, 39, 43, 47, 51) sts onto st holder or waste yarn for shoulder, 75 (73, 73, 77, 77, 81, 81) sts onto a separate st holder or waste yarn for neck, and rem 29 (33, 37, 39, 43, 47, 51) sts onto a third st holder or waste yarn for the other shoulder. Break yarn.

FRONT

Return 125 (133, 141, 149, 157, 165, 173) held front sts to needle and join yarn preparing to work a WS row.

Work in St st, slipping the first st of each row for 7 (7, 7, 9, 9, 11, 11) rows, ending after a WS row.

DIVIDE FOR NECK: (RS) Work as est to 5 sts before center front m, place rem 68 (72, 76, 80, 84, 88, 92) sts onto st holder or waste yarn—57 (61, 65, 69, 73, 77, 81) sts rem for left front. Cont working back and forth on left front sts only.

Shape Left Front Neck

NEXT ROW: (WS) Sl 1 st pwise wyf, purl to end.

DEC ROW: (RS) Sl 1 st pwise wyb, knit to last 3 sts, k2tog, k1—1 st dec'd.

Rep the last 2 rows 27 (27, 27, 29, 29, 29, 29) more times—29 (33, 37, 39, 43, 47, 51) sts rem.

Join Left Shoulder

Break yarn, leaving an 8" (20.5 cm) tail. Transfer left front sts onto a dpn to prepare for grafting. Transfer held 29 (33, 37, 39, 43, 47, 51) sts from back left onto a dpn and use 8" (20.5 cm) tail to graft left front to back sts using Kitchener st (see Glossary).

Shape Right Front Neck

Return 68 (72, 76, 80, 84, 88, 92) held front sts to needle and join yarn preparing to work a RS row.

NEXT ROW: (RS) K11, place these 11 sts onto st holder or waste yarn, knit to end—57 (61, 65, 69, 73, 77, 81) sts rem.

NEXT ROW: (WS) Sl 1 st pwise wyf, purl to end.

DEC ROW: (RS) Sl 1 st pwise wyb, ssk, knit to end—1 st dec'd.

Rep the last 2 rows 27 (27, 27, 29, 29, 29, 29) more times—29 (33, 37, 39, 43, 47, 51) sts rem.

Join Right Shoulder

Break yarn, leaving an 8" (20.5 cm) tail. Transfer right front sts onto a dpn to prepare for grafting. Transfer held 29 (33, 37, 39, 43, 47, 51) sts from back right onto dpn and using 8" (20.5 cm) tail to graft right front to back sts using Kitchener st.

FINISHING

Block piece to measurements.

Armbands

Return 12 held underarm sts from one armhole to dpn, with RS facing and using dpn, pick up and knit 63 (63, 63, 69, 69, 71, 71) sts evenly around armhole selvedge edge, k6 to center of underarm sts, pm for beg of rnd—75 (75, 75, 81, 81, 83, 83) sts.

INC RND: K7, [yo, k1] to last 6 sts, k6—137 (137, 137, 149, 149, 153, 153) sts.

Change to shorter cir needle and knit 4 rnds.

BO all sts loosely.

Work second armband the same as the first.

Neckband

Return 11 held center front sts to shorter cir needle, with RS facing, pick up and knit 28 (28, 28, 30, 30, 30, 30) sts along right front selvedge edge, pm, return 75 (73, 73, 77, 77, 81, 81) held back neck sts to empty end of needle and knit across, pm, pick up and knit 28 (28, 28, 30, 30, 30, 30) sts along left front selvedge edge, pm for beg of rnd—142 (140, 140, 148, 148, 152, 152) sts.

INC RND: K11, [yo, k1] to m, sl m, knit to next m, sl m, [k1, yo] to end of rnd—198 (196, 196, 208, 208, 212, 212) sts.

Knit 4 rnds.

BO all sts loosely.

Using tapestry needle, weave in all ends neatly.

Block again if desired.

LATHAM *gansey jacket*

A stranded gansey jacket is the ultimate in classic comfort. This piece can be worn as a light jacket during transitional seasons; however, because it's not too thick or bulky, it can also be worn under a heavy coat in the cold, wintry months. Men often avoid bold patterns, textures, or colors, so I've chosen to consolidate the pattern at the bottom and leave the upper part of the sweater very simple and clean. This piece is worked bottom up in the round with steeks.

finished size

About 39¼ (42, 44¾, 47¾, 50½, 54¼, 55¼)" (99.5 [106.5, 113.5, 121.5, 128.5, 138, 140.5] cm) chest circumference, buttoned with 2½" (6.5 cm) overlapping buttonband.

Cardigan shown measures 44¾" (113.5 cm).

yarn

Worsted (#4 Medium).

SHOWN HERE: Brooklyn Tweed Shelter (100% Targhee Columbia wool; 140 yd [128 m]/3/4 oz [50 g]): #19 postcard (A), 8 (9, 9, 10, 11, 12, 13) hanks; #16 pumpernickel (B), 1 (1, 2, 2, 2, 2, 2) hanks; #10 birdbrook (C), 1 hank.

needles

Size U.S. 8 (5 mm): 16" (40 cm) and 32" (80 cm) circular (cir), and set of 4 or 5 double-pointed (dpn).

Adjust needle size if necessary to obtain the correct gauge.

notions

Markers (m); stitch holders or waste yarn; tapestry needle; ten 1" (2.5 cm) buttons; sharp scissors; needle and button thread for sewing on buttons.

BUTTONS SHOWN HERE: The Durango Button Co., DH32 Horn Mint (25mm).

gauge

17 sts and 26 rnds = 4" (10 cm) in St st worked in rnds.

notes

- It is recommended to use a contrasting color stitch marker for the steek markers, to easily tell them apart from other markers used.
- The shoulders are joined by using a three-needle bind-off method, with the RS facing. This creates a pronounced seam on the RS of the fabric. Alternatively, the shoulders may be joined with the WS's facing for a hidden seam.

stitch guide

1×1 Rib worked in rows
(multiple of 2 sts)

ROW 1: *K1, p1; rep from *.

ROW 2: *P1, k1; rep from *.

Rep Rows 1 and 2 for patt.

1×1 Rib worked in the round
(multiple of 2 sts)

RND 1: *K1, p1; rep from *.

Rep Rnd 1 for patt.

4 (4½, 5¼, 5¾, 6½, 6¾, 7)"
10 (11.5, 13.5, 14.5, 16.5, 16.5, 18) cm

8½ (8½, 9, 9, 9, 10, 10¼)"
21.5 (21.5, 23, 23, 23, 25.5, 26) cm

20¾ (21¼, 21¾, 22½, 22¾, 23, 23¼)"
55 (56.5, 57.5, 59.5, 60.5, 61, 61.5) cm

7 (7½, 8, 8½, 9, 9½, 10)"
18 (19, 20.5, 21.5, 23, 24, 25.5) cm

10 (10, 10¼, 10¼, 10¾, 11¾, 12¼)"
25.5 (25.5, 26, 26, 27.5, 30, 31) cm

16 (17½, 18½, 19¼, 20¼, 21¾, 22½)"
40.5 (44.5, 47, 49, 51.5, 55, 57) cm

14½ (15, 15½, 16, 16, 16½, 17)"
37 (38, 39.5, 40.5, 40.5, 42, 43) cm

39¼ (42, 44¾, 47¾, 50½, 54¼, 55¼)"
99.5 (106.5, 113.5, 121.5, 128.5, 138, 140.5) cm
with 2½" (6.5 cm) opening on front for band

BODY CHART   SLEEVE CHART

with color A, knit

• with color A, purl

◆ with color B, knit

× with color C, knit

pattern repeat

BODY

Using color A and longer cir needle, CO 164 (180, 188, 204, 212, 228, 236) sts. Place marker (pm) for beg of rnd, and join to work in the rnd, being careful not to twist sts. Beg of rnd m is at the left side of body.

EST RIBBING AND STEEK: P2 (2, 0, 0, 2, 2, 0), [k2, p2] 9 (10, 11, 12, 12, 13, 14) times, pm for steek, k12 for center steek column, pm for steek, [k2, p2] 28 (31, 33, 36, 37, 40, 42) times, k2 (2, 0, 0, 2, 2, 0).

Rep the last rnd until piece meas 1½" (3.8 cm) from CO edge.

Sizes 39¼ (44¾", 50½, 54½)" only

INC RND: K1, M1L (see Glossary), k50 (56, 62, 68) M1R (see Glossary), k1, M1L, knit to end, M1R—168 (192, 216, 240) sts.

Sizes 42 (47¾, 54¼)" only

Knit 1 rnd.

All Sizes

EST BODY CHART: Work Body chart for your size to steek m, taking note of which st of the chart last worked, sl m, work steek sts by alternating the colors, sl m, then cont working the Body chart to end, beg with the following st of the chart.

Cont working Body chart as est until all 58 rnds are completed.

Work St st (knit all sts every rnd) in color A until piece meas 14½ (15, 15½, 16, 16, 16½, 17)" (37 [38, 39.5, 40.5, 40.5, 42, 43] cm) from CO edge.

FRONT

Separate for Front and Work Armholes

NEXT ROW: (RS) K83 (91, 95, 103, 107, 115, 118), place next 10 (10, 10, 10, 10, 10, 12) sts onto st holder or waste yarn for underarm, turn so WS is facing, leaving rem sts unworked for back.

NEXT ROW: (WS) P78 (86, 90, 98, 102, 110, 112), place next 10 (10, 10, 10, 10, 10, 12) sts onto st holder or waste yarn for underarm, turn—78 (86, 90, 98, 102, 110, 112) sts rem for front.

Place 70 (74, 82, 86, 94, 98, 104) back sts onto st holder or waste yarn.

Work even in St st (knit on RS, purl on WS) on front sts only until armholes meas 7 (7½, 8, 8½, 9, 9½, 10)" (18 [19, 20.5, 21.5, 23, 24, 25.5] cm) from divide, ending after a RS row.

NEXT ROW: (WS) P33 (37, 39, 43, 45, 49, 50) place these sts onto st holder or waste yarn for right front, BO 12 steek sts pwise, p33 (37, 39, 43, 45, 49, 50) to end and place these sts onto st holder or waste yarn for left front. Break yarn.

BACK

Armholes

Return 70 (74, 82, 86, 94, 98, 104) held back sts to needle and join color A preparing to work a RS row.

Work even in St st until armhole meas 7 (7½, 8, 8½, 9, 9½, 10)" (18 [19, 20.5, 21.5, 23, 24, 25.5] cm) from divide, ending after a WS row.

Join Shoulders

Transfer 17 (19, 22, 24, 28, 28, 30) sts at armhole edge of right front sts to spare needle, keeping rem 16 (18, 17, 19, 17, 21, 20) sts on holder.

With WS's of back and fronts facing each other, use the three-needle BO (see Glossary) to join 17 (19, 22, 24, 28, 28, 30) right front and back sts for right shoulder. Break yarn.

Place next 36 (36, 38, 38, 38, 42, 44) back sts onto st holder or waste yarn for neck. Transfer 17 (19, 22, 24, 28, 28, 30) sts at armhole edge of held left front sts to spare needle, keeping rem 16 (18, 17, 19, 17; 21, 20) sts on holder. Rejoin yarn and use the three-needle BO to join rem 17 (19, 22, 24, 28, 28, 30) left front and back sts. Break yarn.

SLEEVES

Transfer 10 (10, 10, 10, 10, 10, 12) sts from one underarm to shorter cir needle, then with RS facing and color A, pick up and knit 58 (64, 68, 72, 76, 82, 84) sts, k5 (5, 5, 5, 5, 5, 6), pm for beg of rnd, join to work in the rnd—68 (74, 78, 82, 86, 92, 96) sts.

Work in St st until piece meas 1" (2.5 cm) from pick-up rnd.

Shape Sleeve

note: *Change to dpn when sts no longer fit comfortably on cir needle.*

Knit 3 (2, 2, 2, 3, 2, 3) rnds even.

DEC RND 1: K1, k2tog, knit to last 3 sts, ssk, k1—2 sts dec'd.

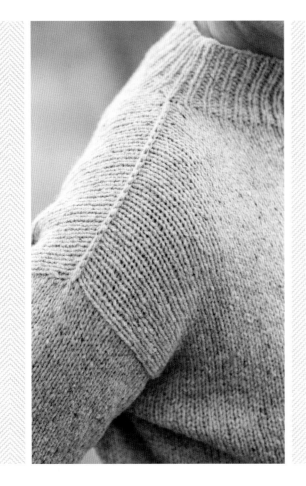

Rep the last 4 (3, 3, 3, 4, 3, 3) rnds 4 (6, 0, 5, 8, 10, 3) times—58 (60, 76, 70, 68, 70, 88) sts rem.

[Knit 4 (3, 3, 3, 4, 3, 4) rnds even, then rep dec rnd 1] 2 (3, 8, 5, 1, 2, 8) time(s)—54 (54, 60, 60, 66, 66, 72) sts rem.

Cont working even in St st until piece meas 8½ (9, 8½, 9¼, 8¾, 9¾, 9¼)" (21.5 [23, 21.5, 23.5, 22, 25, 23.5] cm) from pick-up rnd.

Work Rnds 1–58 of Sleeve chart.

DEC RND 2: K1, k2tog, [k13 (13, 15, 15, 16, 16, 18), k2tog] twice, knit to last 3 sts, ssk, k1—4 sts dec'd.

[Knit 4 rnds, then rep dec rnd 2] 2 (2, 3, 3, 4, 3, 4) times—42 (42, 44, 44, 46, 50, 52) sts rem.

Work even 1x1 rib for 1¾" (4.5 cm).

BO all sts in patt.

Work second sleeve the same as the first.

FINISHING

Complete steek (see Glossary).

Block to measurements.

Buttonband and Collar

With longer cir needle, beg at right front bottom edge, pick up and knit 108 (112, 118, 122, 124, 128, 134) sts evenly along right front to neck edge, pm, place 16 (18, 17, 19, 17, 21, 20) held right front sts, 36 (36, 38, 38, 38, 42, 44) held back neck sts and 16 (18, 17, 19, 17, 21, 20) held left front sts onto empty end of needle then knit across, pm, then pick up and knit 108 (112, 118, 122, 124, 128, 134) sts evenly along left front edge—284 (296, 308, 320, 320, 340, 352) sts.

Work 1 row even in 1x1 rib.

INC ROW 1: (RS) Cont in est 1x1 rib to 1 st before m, k1f&b, sl m, M1L, cont in est 1x1 rib to 1 st before next m, [purl into the front, knit into the back] of the next st, sl m, M1P (see Glossary), cont in est 1x1 rib to end—4 sts inc'd.

Work 1 row even in 1x1 rib.

INC ROW 2: Cont in est 1x1 rib to 1 st before m, [purl into the front, knit into the back] of the next st, sl m, M1P, cont in est 1x1 rib to 1 st before next m, k1f&b, sl m, M1L, cont in est 1x1 rib to end—4 sts inc'd.

Rep the last 4 rows once more—300 (312, 324, 336, 336, 356, 368) sts.

Work 1 row even in 1x1 rib.

BUTTONHOLE ROW: (RS) Work as for inc row 1 to second m, sl m, M1P, work 5 (2, 7, 3, 5, 7, 5) sts in 1x1 rib, yo, k2tog or ssp keeping in patt, *work 9 (10, 10, 11, 11, 11, 12) sts in 1x1 rib, yo, k2tog or ssp keeping in patt; rep from * 8 more times, work in 1x1 rib to end—304 (316, 328, 340, 340, 360, 372) sts.

Work 1 row even in 1x1 rib.

Rep inc row 2—308 (320, 332, 344, 344, 364, 376) sts.

Work 1 row even in 1x1 rib.

Rep inc row 1—312 (324, 336, 348, 348, 368, 380) sts.

Work 1 row even in 1x1 rib.

BO all sts in patt.

Using needle and button thread, sew buttons onto band so that they line up with buttonholes.

Using tapestry needle, weave in all ends neatly.

Block again if desired.

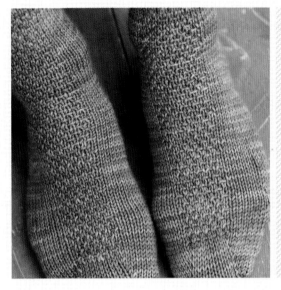

CUFF-TO-CUFF *socks* ⌘

There are few things I dread more than knitting a second (insert garment). We knitters have attacked the problem head-on by creating two-at-a-time techniques and magic-loop methods. Because I love knitted socks, I've tried every method and mantra to get myself hyped up about sock number two. I finally decided to take a stab at the "sock-uation." I realized it would be easy to keep on track if I didn't have to cast on and bind off twice, and the cuff-to-cuff method was born!

finished size

CIRCUMFERENCE: About 5¾ (6½, 7, 8)" (14.5 [16.5, 18, 20.5] cm).

FOOT LENGTH: About 5¾ (7, 7, 7¾)" (14.5 [18, 18, 19.5] cm).

TO FIT: 5–8y (7–10y, Women's U.S. sizes 6–9, Women's U.S. sizes 8–11).

Socks shown measure 5¾" (14.5 cm) and 8" (20.5 cm).

yarn

DK (#3 Light).

SHOWN HERE: Tanis Fiber Arts Yellow Label DK (100% superwash merino wool; 260 yd [238 m]/115 g): sprout, 1 (1, 1, 2) hanks.

needles

Size U.S. 6 (4 mm): Two 16" (40 cm) circular (cir) and set of 2 double-pointed (dpn).

Adjust needle size if necessary to obtain the correct gauge.

notions

Markers (m); waste yarn; tapestry needle.

gauge

25 sts and 34 rnds = 4" (10 cm) in St st, worked in rnds.

notes

✳ These socks are worked by casting on at one cuff, and the first sock is completed cuff-down with a no-wrap short-row heel. The toe is shaped before working scrap yarn (to be removed later). Rejoin yarn and begin second sock starting at the toe. It is completed toe-up with a no-wrap short-row heel. Remove scrap yarn and graft toes closed. (See Separating Toes on page 126.)

✳ For men's U.S. sizes 8½–10 socks, add ½" (1.3 cm) length to the leg and foot when knitting the women's U.S. sizes 6–9.

✳ For men's U.S. sizes 10½–12 socks, add ½" (1.3 cm) length to the leg and 1" (2.5 cm) to the foot when knitting the women's U.S. sizes 8–11.

stitch guide

1×1 Rib *(multiple of 2 sts)*

RND 1: *K1, p1; rep from *.

Rep Rnd 1 for patt.

Elastic Bind-Off

*K2tog tbl, transfer the new stitch from the right needle back to the left needle; repeat from * to end. Break yarn and thread tail through last stitch pulling tight to secure.

WOVEN CHART

3

1

☐ knit

⊻ sl 1 st pwise wyf

☐ pattern repeat

FIRST SOCK

Top-Down Leg

CO 36 (40, 44, 50) sts. Divide sts over 2 cir needles, place marker (pm) for beg of rnd and join to work in the rnd, being careful not to twist sts.

note: "Needle 1" holds the first 18 (20, 22, 24) sts for the front/instep; "needle 2" holds the last 18 (20, 22, 26) sts for the back/heel.

Work in 1x1 rib until piece meas 1" (2.5 cm) from CO edge.

Knit 1 rnd.

EST PATT: Needle 1: k4 (5, 6, 7), pm, work 10 sts in Woven chart, pm, knit to end of needle 1; needle 2: knit.

Cont working even as est until piece meas 6 (6½, 7, 7½)" (15 [16.5, 18, 19] cm) from CO edge, ending last rnd after Rnd 3 of Woven chart is worked on needle 1; do not work sts on needle 2.

Top-Down Heel

Heel is shaped by working no-wrap short-rows (see Glossary) back and forth over needle 2 only as foll:

SHORT-ROW 1: (RS) Sl 1 st purlwise with yarn in back (pwise wyb), knit to last st, turn so WS is facing; (WS) sl 1 st pwise wyf, purl to last st, turn so RS is facing.

SHORT-ROW 2: Sl 1 st pwise wyb, knit to 1 st before gap, turn so WS is facing; (WS) sl 1 st pwise wyf, purl to 1 st before gap, turn so RS is facing.

Rep the last short-row 4 (5, 5, 8) more times.

NEXT ROW: (RS) Sl 1 st pwise wyb, knit to end of needle 2, closing gaps as you come to them.

NEXT RND: Work across needle 1 in patt and knit to end of needle 2, closing rem gaps as you come to them.

Top-Down Foot

Cont working even as est until piece meas 4½ (5½, 5½, 6)" (11.5 [14, 14, 15] cm) from back of heel, or 1¼ (1½, 1½, 1¾)" (3.2 [3.8, 3.8, 4.5] cm) shorter than desired total length.

Remove markers for Woven chart on the last rnd.

Top-Down Toe

SET-UP RND: Needle 1: K6 (7, 7, 8), pm, k6 (6, 8, 8), pm, k6 (7, 7, 8); needle 2: k6 (7, 7, 9), pm, k6 (6, 8, 8), pm, k6 (7, 7, 9).

Shape Toe

DEC RND: *Knit to 2 sts before m, ssk, sl m, knit to m, sl m, k2tog, knit to end of needle; rep from * for needle 2—4 sts dec'd.

NEXT RND: Knit.

Rep the last 2 rnds 4 (5, 5, 6) more times—16 (16, 20, 22) sts rem.

Break yarn, leaving 8" (20.5 cm) tail.

Join waste yarn and knit 3 rnds.

SECOND SOCK

Toe-Up Toe

Rejoin working yarn, leaving 8" (20.5 cm) tail.

Knit 2 rnds.

Shape Toe

NEXT RND: Knit.

INC RND: *Knit to m, M1R (see Glossary), sl m, knit to m, sl m, M1L (see Glossary), knit to end of needle; rep from * for needle 2—4 sts inc'd.

Rep the last 2 rnds 4 (5, 5, 6) more times—36 (40, 44, 50) sts.

Remove markers for toe on the last rnd.

Toe-Up Foot

EST PATT: Needle 1: k4 (5, 6, 7), pm, work 10 sts in Woven chart, pm, knit to end of needle 1; needle 2: knit.

Cont working even as est until piece meas 4¼ (5¼, 5¼, 5½)" (11 [13.5, 13.5, 14] cm) from beg of toe, or 1½ (1¾, 1¾, 2¼)" (3.8 [4.5, 4.5, 5.5] cm) less than total desired length, ending last rnd after Row 1 of Woven chart is worked on needle 1; do not work sts on needle 2.

Toe-Up Heel

Work same as for top-down heel.

Toe-Up Leg

Cont working even as est until piece meas 5 (5½, 6, 6½)" (12.5 [14, 15, 16.5] cm) from end of heel shaping.

Work in 1x1 rib for 1" (2.5 cm).

BO all sts using elastic bind-off (see Stitch Guide).

FINISHING

Remove waste yarn from between toes and use 8" (20.5 cm) tail to graft toe sts together (see Separating Toes on page 126). Block to measurements. Weave in ends.

SEPARATING TOES

Here's how to cut your sock tube and finish your toes to create a perfect pair. Using sharp scissors, carefully cut across waste yarn along the second round of waste yarn stitches *(Figure 1)*. You now have two separate socks *(Figure 2)*. Remove waste yarn between toes and place sts onto 2 dpn so that top sts are on one needle and bottom sts are on one needle, redistributing as needed so each needle has the same number of sts *(Figure 3)*. Using 8" (20.5 cm) tail and tapestry needle, graft toe sts together using Kitchener st *(Figure 4; see Glossary)*.

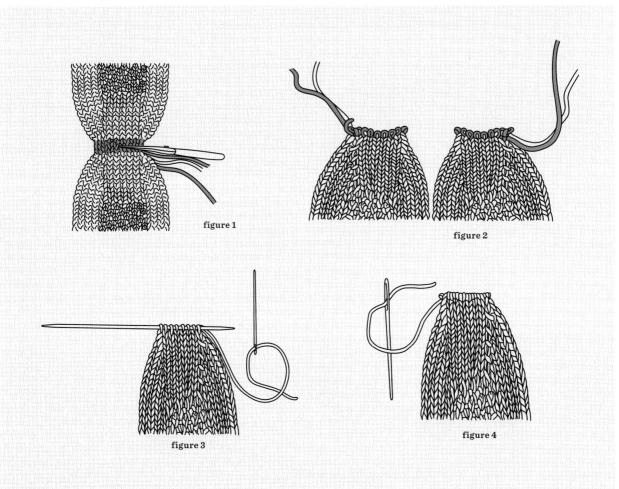

figure 1

figure 2

figure 3

figure 4

ABBREVIATIONS

[ ]	Repeat instructions within brackets as written.
( )	Alternate instructions within parenthesis.
beg	Begin/beginning
cir	Circular
cm	Centimeter(s)
cn	Cable needle
CO	Cast on
cont	Continue
dec(s)('d)	Decrease(s)(d)
dpn	Double-pointed needle(s)
est	Establish(ed)
foll	Follow(ing)
inc(s)('d)	Increase(s)(d)
k	Knit
k2tog	Knit 2 stitches together; one stitch decreased.
k1f&b	Knit into the front and back of stitch; one stitch increased.
kwise	Knitwise
m	Marker
m1	Make 1 stitch; right or left slanting increase as indicated by R/L using the lifted bar increase method.

meas	Measure(s)
p	Purl
patt	Pattern
pm	Place marker
p2tog	Purl 2 stitches together; one stitch decreased.
pwise	Purlwise
rem	Remain(ing)
rep	Repeat(s)
rnd(s)	Round(s)
rS	Right side
sl	Slip
ssk	Slip, slip, knit slipped stitches together; one stitch decreased.
st(s)	Stitch(es)
tbl	Through back loop
WS	Wrong side
wyb	With yarn in back
wyf	With yarn in front
yo	Yarn over

GLOSSARY

BIND-OFFS

Standard Bind-Off

Knit the first stitch, *knit the next stitch (two stitches on right needle), insert left needle tip into first stitch on right needle *(Figure 1)* and lift this stitch up and over the second stitch *(Figure 2)* and off the needle *(Figure 3)*. Repeat from * for the desired number of stitches.

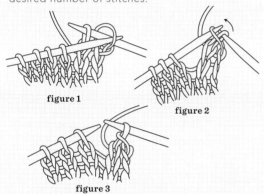

figure 1

figure 2

figure 3

Three-Needle Bind-Off

Place the stitches to be joined onto two separate needles and hold the needles parallel so that the right sides (or wrong sides, if specified in pattern) of knitting face together. Insert a third needle into the first stitch on each of two needles *(Figure 1)* and knit them together as one stitch *(Figure 2)*, *knit the next stitch on each needle the same way, then use the left needle tip to lift the first stitch over the second and off the needle *(Figure 3)*. Repeat from * until no stitches remain on first two needles. Cut yarn and pull tail through last stitch to secure.

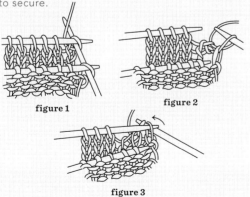

figure 1

figure 2

figure 3

CAST-ONS

Backward-Loop Cast-On

*Loop working yarn and place it on needle backward so that it doesn't unwind. Repeat from *.

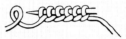

Cable Cast-On

If there are no stitches on the needles, make a slipknot of working yarn and place it on the left needle, then use the knitted method to cast on one more stitch—two stitches on needle. When there are at least two stitches on the left needle, hold needle with working yarn in your left hand. *Insert right needle between the first two stitches on left needle *(Figure 1)*, wrap yarn around needle as if to knit, draw yarn through *(Figure 2)*, and place new loop on left needle *(Figure 3)* to form a new stitch. Repeat from * for the desired number of stitches, always working between the first two stitches on the left needle.

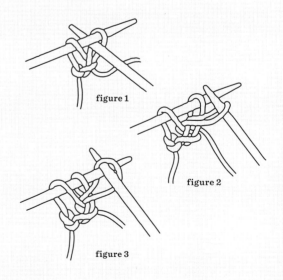

figure 1

figure 2

figure 3

Long-Tail (Continental) Cast-On

Leaving a long tail (about ½" [1.3 cm] for each stitch to be cast on), make a slipknot and place on right needle. Place thumb and index finger of your left hand between the yarn ends so that working yarn is around your index finger and tail end is around your thumb and secure the yarn ends with your other fingers. Hold your palm upward, making a V of yarn *(Figure 1)*. *Bring needle up through loop on thumb *(Figure 2)*, catch first strand around index finger, and go back down through loop on thumb *(Figure 3)*. Drop loop off thumb and, placing thumb back in V configuration, tighten resulting stitch on needle *(Figure 4)*. Repeat from * for the desired number of stitches.

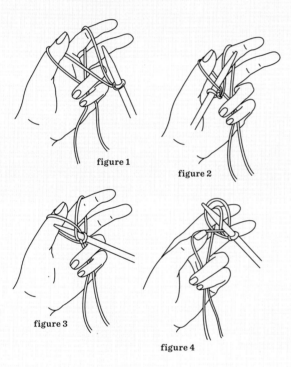

figure 1

figure 2

figure 3

figure 4

Two-Needle Cast-On

This handy cast-on is a simple long-tail cast-on that places stitches onto two different needles (or two ends of a circular needle) at once. From there you can knit in the round (as for toe-up socks), flat from one needle to the other, or flat working straight out from each needle separately.

STEP 1. Make a slipknot, leaving a tail long enough to cast on the desired number of stitches. Holding a circular needle so the points are parallel and held to the left with the cord to the right, place the slip-knot on the needle farthest from you *(Figure 1)*.

STEP 2. As with the long-tail cast-on, hold the tail yarn over the thumb and the yarn from the ball over the index finger. Bring the ball-side yarn forward, over the needle nearest you, and down between the two needles. There is now one stitch on each needle *(Figure 2)*.

STEP 3. Bring tail yarn away from you, over the far needle, and down between the two needles. There are now three stitches on the needles: two on the far needle and one on the near needle *(Figure 3)*.

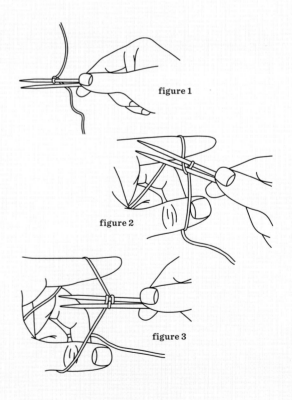

figure 1

figure 2

figure 3

STEP 4. Bring the ball-side yarn forward, over the needle nearest you, and down between the two needles *(Figure 4)*.

Repeat Steps 3 and 4 until you've cast on the desired number of stitches. To begin knitting, bring the tail yarn along the back of the cast-on stitches around the ball-side yarn, twisting the two stitches *(Figure 5)*. Rotate the needles to the right so that the far needle is now the right needle. Slide the right needle forward so that stitches are on the cable and, using ball-side yarn, knit the first stitch on the left needle *(Figure 6)*.

The wrong side of the work is shown here.

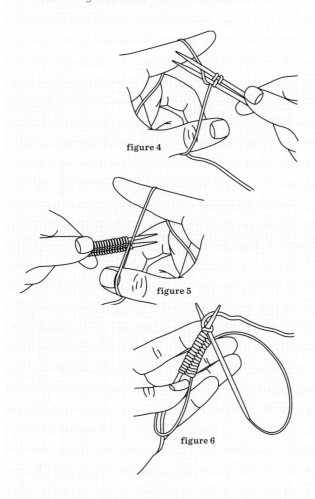

figure 4

figure 5

figure 6

DECREASES

Knit 2 Together (k2tog)

Knit two stitches together as if they were a single stitch.

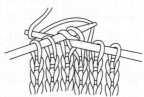

Knit 2 Together Through the Back Loop (k2tog-tbl)

Insert needle into back loop of two stitches and knit together as if they were a single stitch.

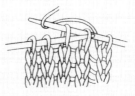

Purl 2 Together (p2tog)

Purl two stitches together as if they were a single stitch.

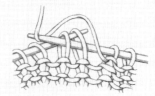

Slip, Slip, Knit (ssk)

Slip two stitches individually knitwise (*Figure 1*), insert left needle tip into the front of these two slipped stitches, and use the right needle to knit them together through their back loops (*Figure 2*).

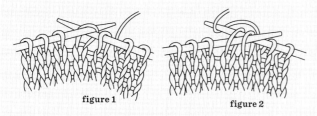

figure 1   figure 2

Slip, Slip, Purl (ssp)

Holding yarn in front, slip two stitches knitwise one at a time onto right needle (*Figure 1*). Slip them back onto left needle and purl the two stitches together through back loops (*Figure 2*).

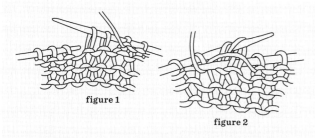

figure 1

figure 2

Joining for Working in Rounds

For projects that begin with ribbing or stockinette st, simply arrange the stitches for working in rounds, then knit the first stitch that was cast on to form a tube.

For projects that begin with seed, garter, or reverse stockinette st, arrange the needle so that the yarn tail is at the left needle tip. Holding the yarn in back, slip the first st from the right needle onto the left needle (*Figure 1*), bring the yarn to the front between the two needles, and slip the first two stitches from the left tip to the right tip (*Figure 2*), then bring the yarn to the back between the two needles and slip the first stitch from the right tip to the left tip (*Figure 3*).

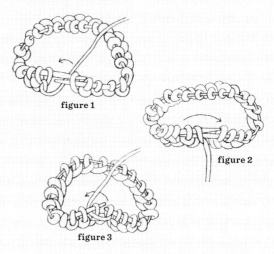

figure 1

figure 2

figure 3

I-CORD
(Also called Knit-Cord)

With double-pointed needle, cast on desired number of stitches. *Without turning the needle, slide the stitches to other end of the needle, pull the yarn around the back, and knit the stitches as usual; repeat from * for desired length.

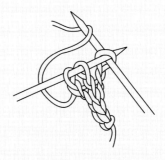

INCREASES

Bar Increase (k1f&b)

Knit into a stitch but leave the stitch on the left needle *(Figure 1)*, then knit through the back loop of the same stitch *(Figure 2)* and slip the original stitch off the needle *(Figure 3)*.

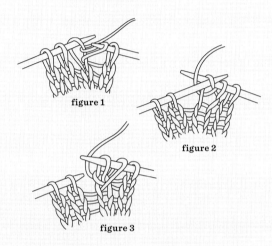

figure 1

figure 2

figure 3

Raised Make-One (M1) Increase

note: Use the left slant if no direction of slant is specified.

Left Slant (M1L)

With left needle tip, lift the strand between the last knitted stitch and the first stitch on the left needle from front to back *(Figure 1)*, then knit the lifted loop through the back *(Figure 2)*.

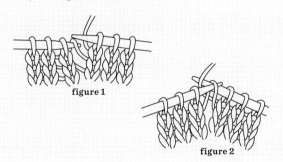

figure 1

figure 2

Right Slant (M1R)

With left needle tip, lift the strand between the needles from back to front *(Figure 1)*. Knit the lifted loop through the front *(Figure 2)*.

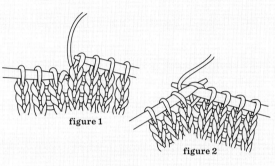

figure 1

figure 2

Purlwise (M1P)

With left needle tip, lift the strand between the needles from front to back *(Figure 1)*, then purl the lifted loop through the back *(Figure 2)*.

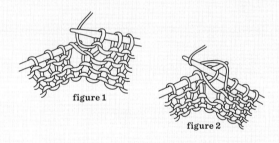

figure 1

figure 2

GRAFTING

Kitchener Stitch

This useful technique can be difficult for a beginner simply because of the number of steps and the order in which the stitches are worked. However, once you learn the pattern and get into the rhythm of the stitching, you'll find that grafting can go very quickly and smoothly. I recommend knitting two swatches and placing the live stitches on double-pointed needles so you can practice the technique before moving on to your garment.

Arrange stitches on two needles so that there is an equal number of stitches on each needle. Hold the needles parallel to each other with wrong sides of the knitting together. Allowing about ½" (1.3 cm) per stitch to be grafted, thread matching yarn on a tapestry needle. Work from right to left as follows:

STEP 1. Bring tapestry needle through the first stitch on the front needle as if to purl and leave the stitch on the needle *(Figure 1)*.

STEP 2. Bring tapestry needle through the first stitch on the back needle as if to knit and leave that stitch on the needle *(Figure 2)*.

STEP 3. Bring tapestry needle through the first front stitch as if to knit and slip this stitch off the needle. Then bring tapestry needle through the next front stitch as if to purl and leave this stitch on the needle *(Figure 3)*.

STEP 4. Bring tapestry needle through the first back stitch as if to purl and slip this stitch off the needle. Then bring tapestry needle through the next back stitch as if to knit and leave this stitch on the needle *(Figure 4)*.

Repeat Steps 3 and 4 until one stitch remains on each needle, adjusting the tension to match the rest of the knitting as you go. To finish, bring tapestry needle through the front stitch as if to knit and slip this stitch off the needle. Then bring tapestry needle through the back stitch as if to purl and slip this stitch off the needle.

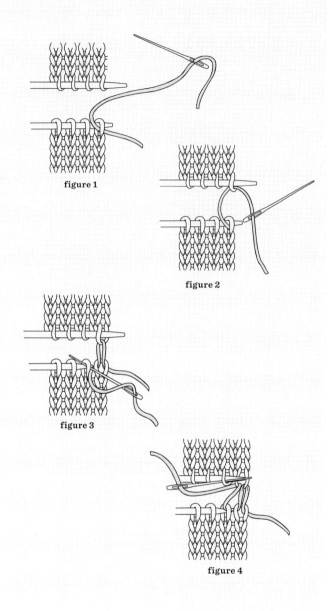

figure 1

figure 2

figure 3

figure 4

No-Wrap Short-Rows

These short-rows are quick and simple and lack the tension problems many knitters face with wrapped short-rows. Create the short-rows as instructed in the pattern, remembering to slip your stitches purlwise at the start of each short-row and working from the right or wrong side of the knitting. You will notice a substantial gap at each slipped stitch. Here's how to close the gaps quickly and easily.

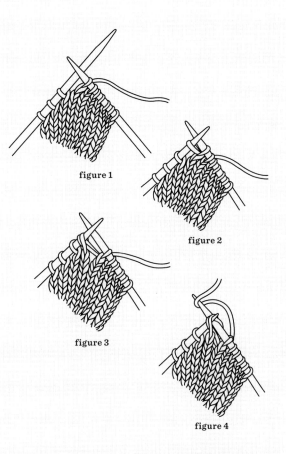

figure 1

figure 2

figure 3

figure 4

Knit Side Facing

STEP 1. Work to the first gap on the left needle. You will see the slipped stitch positioned around the next stitch on the needle (*Figure 1*).

STEP 2. Using the right needle, pick up the slipped stitch (*Figure 2*).

STEP 3. Transfer the slipped stitch onto the left needle (*Figure 3*).

STEP 4. Knit the two stitches together through the back loop (tbl; *Figure 4*).

Purl Side Facing

STEP 1. Work to the first gap on the left needle. You will see the slipped stitch positioned around the next stitch on the needle.

STEP 2. Using the right needle, pick up the slipped stitch.

STEP 3. Transfer the slipped stitch back onto the left needle.

STEP 4. Purl the two stitches together.

Pick Up and Knit

Along CO or BO Edge

With right side facing and working from right to left, insert the tip of the needle into the center of the stitch below the bind-off or cast-on edge (*Figure 1*), wrap yarn around needle, and pull through a loop (*Figure 2*). Pick up one stitch for every existing stitch.

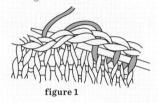

figure 1

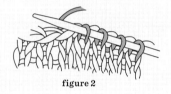

figure 2

Along Side Edge

With right side facing and working from right to left, insert tip of needle between last and second-to-last stitches, wrap yarn around needle, and pull through a loop. Pick up and knit about three stitches for every four rows, adjusting as necessary so that picked-up edge lays flat.

Pom-poms

Pom-poms are an optional embellishment that can add an unexpected pop of color or a dash of whimsy. I have tried every pom-pom maker on the market and some DIY ones, but found them all too fussy and clumsy to work with. This is a new take on pom-pom construction that gives you the freedom to make a pom-pom in virtually any size, and it is a tighter finished piece that won't lose center threads—common problem with many other pom-pom construction techniques.

You will need one rectangular piece of cardboard or cardstock (a business card is a great size for your typical 11" to 1½" (2.5-3.8 cm) finished pom-pom); about 5 g of yarn of your choice; button thread or any other thread that will hold up to pulling tight without breaking; darning needle; scissors.

STEP 1. Hold your cardboard piece horizontally with one hand and begin winding the yarn around the card with the other for about 100 wraps—the more you wrap, the fuller the pom-pom will be—and leave about a 3" (7.5 cm) tail. Once you've finished wrapping, break the yarn leaving a second 3" (7.5 cm) tail and tie the two tails together.

STEP 2. Using the darning needle and button thread, insert the needle between the yarn and the card on the front side and tie the wraps together with the button thread as tightly as possible; repeat on the back side. Slide the yarn off the card. You now have a thick loop of wraps with two points tied securely.

STEP 3. Using another piece of button thread, pinch the two tied points of the loop and tie the loop closed as tightly as possible at the tied points. You now have a pinched loop with a small loop at either side of the center.

STEP 4. Cut the two small loops and trim into a nice fluffy pom-pom.

Steeks

Steeking is possibly the most nerve-wrecking task for a knitter to perform. The idea of any sharp object coming in contact with handknits is chilling, so intentionally putting shears to stitches seems like downright madness. As with most unfamiliar techniques, I recommend trying your hand on a swatch before moving on to a full-size garment.

STEP 1. Locate the center column of stitches; this will be your steek column. Using a contrasting color yarn or thread and tapestry needle, loosely weave through the center of the center steek stitch to mark the st that will be cut *(Figure 1)*.

STEP 2. Using either a needle and thread and small stitches or a sewing machine on a small stitch setting, sew a line straight into the center of the stitches up the columns on either side of your center steek stitch *(Figure 2)*.

STEP 3. Remove contrasting color waste yarn. Using very sharp scissors, carefully cut straight up the steek column *(Figure 3)*.

STEP 4: Fold the extra steeking fabric over to the back side of the knitting and, using matching yarn and a tapestry needle, carefully tack down the cut edge to the back of the knitting using either a whipstitch or blanket stitch.

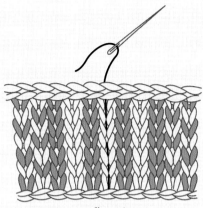

figure 1

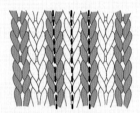

figure 2

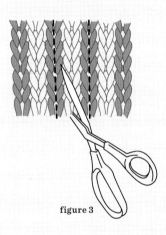

figure 3

TOOLS

All knitters have tool preferences unique to them. Here is some insight into my personal arsenal of must-haves.

NEEDLES

Of all the tools in a knitter's arsenal, needles are clearly the most important. They are available in a variety of materials and styles; each suited for a particular task. For this book, I have primarily used circular and double-pointed needles. The cost for the various needle gauges and cord lengths can add up quickly, so I recommend investing in an interchangeable set, which will ultimately be more affordable and will put (nearly) every point and cable size needed at your fingertips.

YARN NEEDLES

Yarn needles, sometimes referred to as tapestry needles, are available in various lengths, diameters, with bent tips, or straight tips. These handy little tools are essential for finishing tasks such as weaving in ends, seaming, and grafting.

CABLE NEEDLES

Cable needles are available in multiple diameters and bent or hook styles; however, no matter what style or gauge I've used I've always found them clumsy to work with. The job of the cable needle is simply to hold stitches momentarily so that you can rearrange the working order of the stitches by crossing them. If you don't have a cable needle on hand or have trouble handling them, I recommend using a 3″ or 4″ (7.5 or 10 cm) double-pointed needle instead.

STITCH MARKERS

Markers are small rings placed on the needle between stitches. There are many types of markers on the market. This book has patterns that call for removable markers or contrasting markers. Removable markers are open or have a clasp; safety pins make great substitutes. A contrasting marker is simply a marker that will give you a visual cue; it may be a different color, style, or size from the other markers used.

STITCH HOLDERS/WASTE YARN

Stitch holders or waste yarn are used when you need to put aside a group of live stitches. The most common use is for holding sleeve stitches when working a sweater in the round from the top down.

STEEKING SCISSORS

Steeking scissors have very sharp pointed blades that are only about 1″ (2.5 cm) long. These tiny snips are used primarily for cutting the steek in stranded knitting. You can use other sharp scissors, but if you're planning to make a number of projects with steeks, it's worth investing in a pair of steeking scissors.

CHOOSING YARNS

Selecting yarn for a project is the most personal touch any knitter can add to a piece. A pattern is your canvas, and the yarn is your paint.

Having a background in fine art greatly influences the way I see yarn and color. When I first began knitting I realized early on that each fiber is as different as each paint, and even if you've never seen a tube of paint in your life, I'm sure you have some understanding that watercolor is not the same as oil. Within the broad term "oil" there are major differences in stickiness, opacity, and thickness, just as Shetland, Highland, or Merino are all "wool" with completely different textures as the result of climate, fiber length, and stickiness. I could easily ramble on about all the aspects of yarn, but there are two topics in particular I will focus on here: yarn substitution and using hand-dyed yarns.

When designing these projects I spent months toiling over yarn for each piece based on four major factors: weight, fiber content, drape, and color. I understand that substitution is sometimes an inevitable part of knitting, so finding a yarn with the same weight and fiber content is the best way to start; medium-weight cotton is not going to behave like lightweight alpaca and will change the look and feel of the finished piece. Cost may also factor in which yarn you select for a project. I admit I've held a pile of hanks in one hand while nibbling down the nails of the other trying to process and justify a car payment worth of yarn to myself. As I've mentioned, a garment looks the way it does not only because of the fit or stitches used, but because of the recommended yarn's specific properties, so doing a little research on the recommended yarn will help significantly when you begin your search for a substitute. It can be a little overwhelming with all the different blends and ply types available these days, so take advantage of the folks at your local yarn store; they should be able to offer assistance if you feel like you're in over your head and going down the proverbial rabbit hole.

With all of that said, there is still the topic of color. Choosing a color that suits the recipient of the garment is crucial. Women are a little more daring with color and texture, while men can be extremely particular. I can usually choose a yarn that my husband will wear without complaint, but the children are a different story entirely. It's best if you can drag the child you're knitting for along to the yarn store so that he or she can have a hand in selecting the colors. I guide my girls to a section of the store with yarn in suitable weight and fiber for the project and leave them to select color on their own without hovering over them. Even if the little darlings round the corner with an armful of the most hideous color imaginable, if there is a grin on their faces, I dutifully knit it up, knowing they will wear it with pride.

On the topic of hand-dyed yarns, I've actually been forced to bear witness to a public scolding for not alternating hanks of hand-dyed. Certainly it's the universally accepted manner of knitting with the rich, painterly hanks, however, I'm not sure that's the best way to honor the basic nature of the yarn processed in small batches, by hand. The artist in me refuses to alternate hanks in small projects that may require only a single hank to complete because those subtle dashes of light and dark that may pool or streak here and there is why I choose to knit with these yarns. It's a rare and special gift to be able to create something with a material that is, in its own right, a piece of art. If I want a yarn that is colored plain and universally, there are plenty out there for me to choose from in every weight and fiber. The exception is if I'm working up a large piece requiring multiple units of yarn, and especially if I'm using a yarn that either doesn't have dyelots or using yarn of different dyelots is unavoidable. In these situations, one hank of yarn can be drastically different from the next in hue or value, and there will be a visible line across your hard work screaming, "Hey! We don't match!" so alternating hanks is the best way to ensure even color distribution.

BIBLIOGRAPHY

Hiatt, June Hemmons. *Principles of Knitting.* New York: Touchstone, 1988, 2012.

Vogue Knitting. *Stitchionary Volume One.* New York: Sixth & Spring Books, 2005.

Potter Craft. *400 Knitting Stitches.* New York: Potter Craft, 2007.

YARN SOURCES

Artesano Yarns
Artesano Ltd, Unit G, Lambs
Farm Business Park
Basingstoke Rd, Swallowfield
Berkshire, RG7 1PQ, UK, England.
artesanoyarns.co.uk

Briggs and Little
3500 Route 635 Harvey
York County, New Brunswick,
Canada E6K 1J8
(800) 561-9276
briggsandlittle.com

Brooklyn Tweed
brooklyntweed.com

Cephalopod Yarns
1547-B Ridgely St.
Baltimore, MD 21230
(410) 528-8660
cephalopodyarns.com

Classic Elite Yarns
16 Esquire Rd., Unit 2
North Billerica, MA 01862
(800) 343-0308
classiceliteyarns.com

Hikoo
Distributed by Skacel
Collection, Inc.
PO Box 88110
Seattle, WA 98138
(800) 255-1278
skacelknitting.com

Jamieson's of Shetland
Distributed by Simpy Shetland
18375 Olympic Avenue South
Seattle, WA 98188
(877) 743-8526
simplyshetland.net

Madelinetosh
7515 Benbrook Pkwy.
Benbrook, TX 76126
(817) 249-3066
madelinetosh.com

Manos del Uruguay/Fairmount Fibers, Ltd.
PO Box 2082
Philadelphia, PA 19103
(888) 566-9970
fairmountfibers.com

Quince and Co.
32 Main St., Ste. 13-101W
Biddeford, ME 04005
quinceandco.com

Tanis Fiber Arts
tanisfiberarts.com

ACKNOWLEDGMENTS

Most large tasks take many hands, diverse input, and many experts coming together with a common goal, and the writing of this book was not solely my doing. First, I'd like to thank the amazing team at Interweave. Every person I was in contact with throughout the process was a source of support and guidance. This book wouldn't exist without the insight of Kerry Bogert, who has become a great friend and source of inspiration, and I was extremely fortunate to have my editor, Michelle Bredeson, in my corner doing all the heavy lifting.

My family kept my spirits up with love and encouragement—especially my husband, Nate, and my two little girls, Alizah and Maela, who many times had more faith in me than I had in myself. I would be remiss if I didn't thank my mother-in-law, Pam, who sat with me after dinner one night when I was pregnant with my youngest and taught me how to cast on my very first stitch. I'm also blessed to have a large, supportive extended family gently pushing me along. My mother even learned how to knit just so she could help me work on samples.

Special thanks to Mare Pasley, who not only completed nearly all the finishing work for the samples in the book but also made time to visit me regularly (as I'd become more of a shut-in than usual), raise my spirits, raise a glass, and knit anything I tossed in her lap.

I'd also like to thank my team of sample knitters for their distinct role in making sure I had samples to go along with my patterns: Carl P. Bates, Christina Hansen, Chaitanya Muralidhara, Patrice Safarik, and Abigail Warner.

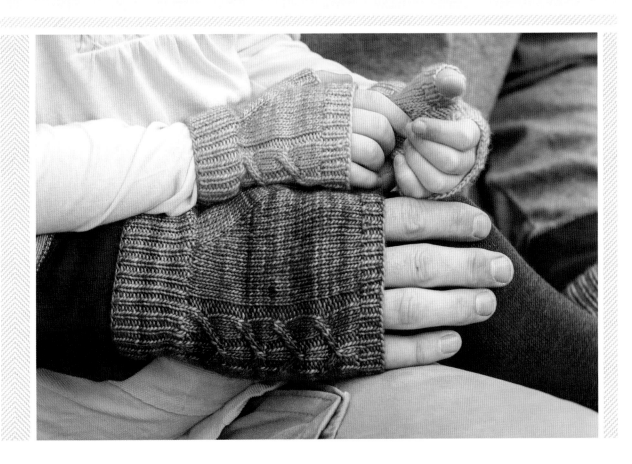

INDEX

To my girls.

I see myself through your eyes and strive every day to be someone you can look up to as a mentor, as your mother, and as a woman of strength and courage.

EDITOR **Michelle Bredeson**

TECHNICAL EDITOR **Kristen TenDyke**

ASSOCIATE ART DIRECTOR **Charlene Tiedemann**

DESIGNER **Karla Baker**

ILLUSTRATOR **Kathie Kelleher**

PHOTOGRAPHER **Joe Hancock**

PHOTO STYLIST **Allie Liebgott**

HAIR AND MAKEUP **Kathy MacKay**

Family-Friendly Knits. Copyright © 2015 by Courtney Spainhower. Manufactured in China. All rights reserved. No part of this book may be reproduced in any form or by any electronic or mechanical means including information storage and retrieval systems without permission in writing from the publisher, except by a reviewer who may quote brief passages in a review. Published by Interweave, an imprint of F+W, A Content + eCommerce Company, 10151 Carver Road, Suite 200, Blue Ash, Ohio 45242. (800) 289-0963. First Edition.

Photography © 2015 Joe Hancock

a content + ecommerce company

www.fwcommunity.com

19 18 17 16 15   5 4 3 2 1

Distributed in Canada by Fraser Direct
100 Armstrong Avenue
Georgetown, ON, Canada L7G 5S4
Tel: (905) 877-4411

Distributed in the U.K. and Europe by F&W
MEDIA INTERNATIONAL
Brunel House, Newton Abbot, Devon, TQ12 4PU,
England
Tel: (+44) 1626 323200, Fax: (+44) 1626 323319
E-mail: enquiries@fwmedia.com

Distributed in Australia by Capricorn Link
P.O. Box 704, S. Windsor NSW, 2756 Australia
Tel: (02) 4560 1600, Fax: (02) 4577 5288
E-mail: books@capricornlink.com.au

SRN: 15KN12
ISBN-13: 978-1-63250-003-8

PDF SRN: EP9576
PDF ISBN-13: 978-1-63250-004-5

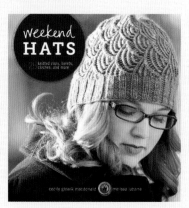
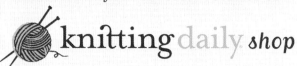
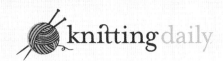